12/03

WITHDRAWN

ACKNOWLEDGMENTS

Writing a book takes considerable time, and that means time away from family and friends. Luckily, I am blessed to be married to a published author whose favorite game is Scrabble and to have a daughter who loves writing as much as I do. This book, like all of my other writing, would not have been possible without their unending patience and understanding for what it means to be a writer. Thank you, Amy and Abigail, for all the love and laughter you have brought to my life.

I am also indebted to my parents and grandparents, who made my childhood years such a joy, and to my five brothers, Bill, Greg, Brian, Andrew, and Anthony, who shared those memorable years with me. I always look forward to spending time together, especially when we all gather for a weekend camping trip or during the holidays. I would not be the person I am today without the support and encouragement of my family.

Also, my friends from college—people like Rob Hendrickson, Steve Kosier, and Michael Handberg—have always been there whenever I reemerge after a long writing project, and my law school classmates, though scattered throughout the country, are never more than a phone call away. To Bruce Beddow in Virginia, Greg Braun in Chicago, Erik Dove in the Twin Cities, and Terry

Anker in Indianapolis, many thanks for your friendship over the years. Katherine Wheaton and Shannon Carlson, two students who helped me gather materials for use in the manuscript, also deserve special thanks, as do Deborah Keenan and Tim Rank, who reviewed the manuscript itself.

One does not become a writer without a little luck and a lot of help. My good fortune started in high school with an English teacher who doubled as my cross-country and track-and-field coach. In exposing me to novels such as Harper Lee's *To Kill a Mockingbird* and Kurt Vonnegut's *Slaughterhouse-Five*, Chris Thiem— like no other teacher—instilled in me a lifelong love of books and language. I will never forget the weekend team runs he led that ended at his house, sometimes followed by a game of Boggle.

Since finishing law school, I have also had the privilege of working with a number of talented lawyers who could have become successful authors had they so chosen. I would be nothing close to the writer I am today if it were not for their guidance and mentoring over the years. My colleagues at Hamline University's M.F.A. program, as well as the dozens of students I have had in my annual seminar at the University of Minnesota Law School, have taught me a great deal too, not only about writing but about the very subject of this book: America's death penalty.

Finally, a special thank you to Bill Frohlich, the director of Northeastern University Press. He agreed to publish this book long before I even wrote the manuscript and, whenever I have been in Boston, he has always shown me and my family wonderful hospitality. Indeed, all the staff at the press, from editor-extraordinaire Ann Twombly to marketing director Jill Bachall to editorial assistant Sarah Rowley, are true professionals who make publishing a book a real delight. A writer could not ask for a better publisher.

The death penalty is an American institution that I cannot stop thinking about, if only because it has shadowed me throughout my life. I grew up in Mankato, Minnesota, where America's largest mass hanging took place, and my childhood home on Mulberry Street is just blocks from the execution site. On a single day in the midst of the Civil War and on President Abraham Lincoln's own orders, thirty-eight Dakota Indians were executed in my hometown on a single gallows. The Native Americans, sentenced to death after perfunctory trials before a military tribunal, were hanged on the day after Christmas in 1862 following the Sioux Uprising, a conflict that claimed hundreds of lives. I was an altar boy at the same Catholic parish that baptized thirty of the condemned Indians before they were put to death. As a boy, I used to ride my bicycle along the Minnesota River to Sibley Park, where—I learned later in life—the condemned men were kept before their execution.[1]

After college at the University of Minnesota, I went to law school in Indiana—a death penalty state. In my first year, I was taught criminal law by Professor Thomas Schornhorst, a fixture at Indiana University in Bloomington who has defended indigent clients in capital cases. He gave me my first taste of the Socratic method, and I still remember him telling graphic stories of kidnappings and murders and war stories from his own cases. One of my later teachers, Joseph Hoffmann, was a former law clerk to U.S. Supreme Court Justice William Rehnquist, the man perhaps most responsible for the recent and severe curtailment of death row inmates' habeas corpus rights.[2]

The death penalty seminar that I took from Professor Hoffmann opened my eyes to what was going on in America's death penalty system and led me to ask why modern-day executions are hidden from public view and often take place in the middle of the night. A paper that I wrote for that class in 1991 gave way to several years of research into that subject and led to the publication of my first book, *Death in the Dark: Midnight Executions in America*.[3]

As a practicing lawyer, I have spent over ten years in a world of day-to-day conflict—civil litigation—and have seen how lawsuits can disrupt, or even destroy, lives. The most memorable of my experiences in the legal profession, though, has involved working on a pro bono basis on death penalty cases venued in Texas. The life-and-death stakes of these cases make them totally unlike the run-of-the-mill commercial disputes that I typically handle.

When one is immersed in a death penalty case, brutal acts of gun violence and murder must be confronted head-on, and one is forced to ask the most fundamental of questions: Why do people kill? What does justice require be done to convicted killers to punish them for their crimes? And what should the role of law be in American society?

I have spent over a decade now thinking about these questions. After finishing my first book, I wrote a second one, *Legacy of Violence: Lynch Mobs and Executions in Minnesota*, which examines the history of executions and lynchings in my home state. Although the State of Minnesota has not executed anyone for decades, I wanted to see how lynchings and executions shaped the history and fabric of life of the place where I live. For the past six years, I have also taught a death penalty course at the University of Minnesota Law School.

Every spring semester my students read about and discuss the complex maze of rules that make up death penalty jurisprudence and debate whether capital punishment should be abolished or retained. As I lead the discussion, I grow only more convinced each year that state-sanctioned killing—what I've come to see as just another form of violence in an already too-violent society—must go the way of lynchings and be relegated to the past. Former New York Governor Mario Cuomo, who favors incarceration over the death penalty, got it right, I think, when he said, "There is a better response to killing than killing."[4]

Four times a year, the NAACP publishes a report called *Death Row U.S.A.* that keeps me abreast of America's death penalty system. The latest report shows that there are 3,718 death row inmates in the United States—3,666 men and 52 women—and thirty-eight states, along with the federal government and the U.S. military, with capital punishment statutes. The District of Columbia and twelve states have no death penalty laws, and these geographically diverse states include Alaska, Hawaii, Maine, Massachusetts, Michigan, Rhode Island, Vermont, and West Virginia. Three of the non–death penalty states—Iowa, North Dakota, and Wisconsin—border Minnesota, which abolished the death penalty in 1911 after a botched hanging of a convicted killer. The list of death penalty states always makes me wonder why some states have resisted reinstating capital punishment, even as places such as Kansas and New York, which once outlawed executions, have recently brought them back.[5]

The NAACP report contains no narrative, just statistics, charts, and references to recent court cases. The report says that, since 1976, 784 executions have taken place in America. Of those executed, all were male except for nine women, Velma Barfield, Karla Faye Tucker, Judy Buenoano, Bettie Lou Beets, Christina Marie Riggs, Lynda Lyon Block, and three offenders—Wanda Jean

Allen, Marilyn Plantz, and Lois Nadean Smith—executed by lethal injection in Oklahoma in 2001. Joe Margulies, Betty Lou Beets's lawyer, has spoken to the students in my seminar about how his client, a sixty-two-year-old great-grandmother, died on a Texas gurney. Joe's vivid description of her execution by lethal injection has stayed with me: his client looked at him, expelled her last breath, and then violently heaved against the gurney's straps as the life went out of her.[6]

The latest NAACP report also shows that more whites than blacks have been executed—whites account for 56 percent of the executions—but that over half of all condemned inmates are minorities. The raw numbers tell me that the murder victim's race and the murder's locale—as opposed to the nature of the crime itself—usually determines who lives and who dies. The NAACP's statistics show that of the crimes that resulted in the nation's 784 executions, over 80 percent of the victims were white and less than 14 percent were black. White-on-white homicides led to 412 executions and black-on-white killings resulted in 176 executions, whereas white-on-black murders account for twelve executions, or less than 2 percent of the total number. The report makes clear that over 65 percent of American executions take place in just five states, Texas, Virginia, Missouri, Florida, and Oklahoma.[7]

This book—part memoir, part essay, and part a telling of true stories—represents the culmination of my thinking about the death penalty. Capital punishment is an emotionally charged issue, and it cannot be honestly considered without taking into account the real human cost of murder and violence. Every time a murderer takes a life, a mother and father's son or daughter is taken from them and cannot be brought back; a life has been snuffed out, and the murder victim's friends and family must abruptly grapple with feelings of loss, rage, and depression. Nor can the issue of the death penalty be fairly discussed without talking about, and addressing head-on, the events of September 11, 2001: unparalleled acts of terrorism occurring right on American soil.

The September 11th terrorist attacks in New York City, at the Pentagon, and on board an airline flight destined to crash into a Pennsylvania field changed America and the world forever. Thousands of lives were taken, the families of police officers, firefighters, airline passengers and office workers lost parents, spouses and loved ones, and the economy fell into a recession. Indeed, after two commercial jets were piloted into New York's tallest skyscrapers, it wasn't long before American troops were dispatched to Afghanistan to fight the Taliban regime, which refused to turn over Osama bin Laden and members of the Al Qaeda terrorist network.

Criminal acts, whether committed in New York or in our own neighborhoods, have a profound impact on American life. The fear they engender causes some people to stop flying or, in crime-ridden areas, to stay indoors out of a concern over stray gunfire. The sniper shootings in the Washington, D.C., area in the fall of 2002 literally brought freeway traffic to a near standstill as police officers tried to solve the case and apprehend those responsible. When terrorists or murderers take lives, they do irreparable damage by callously inflicting human suffering. How could any thinking person do anything other than recoil in horror at the sight of smoke billowing from the World Trade Center towers and office workers plummeting hundreds of feet to their deaths? What deadly drive-by shooting on a neighborhood block could conceivably not affect the lives of that street's residents?

Although the tragic events of September 11th changed us all, I do not believe those events should be allowed to dictate the outcome of America's death penalty debate. The issue to be debated, after all, is not whether terrorists and murderers have committed despicable acts of violence; we can all agree that they have. Instead, it is whether executions serve any worthwhile or legitimate purpose. The question we must ask ourselves is this: after a

homicide or mass murder has occurred and the criminal is in custody, what will our response as Americans be? At least if one con-
siders 2002 polling data showing little change in people's views
on the death penalty after that unforgettable day, Americans' attitudes toward the death penalty have not been materially affected.
Indeed, in the post–September 11th era, significant legislative and
judicial activity has already taken place that either halts executions in a particular locale or imposes restrictions on how or
when the death penalty can be imposed.[8]

Over fifteen years ago, when I attended Mankato's Loyola High
School, I used to think about capital punishment in fairly simplis-
tic terms, focusing on the "deterrence" issue. I remember seeing
conflicting statistical studies, some claiming death sentences deter violent crime and others finding executions had no greater deterrent effect than life sentences. Today, I no longer see the death
penalty as a contest between conflicting studies or, for that matter, as some abstract public policy debate, as it remains for some.
I have met people whose family members have been murdered
and I have seen America's capital punishment system in operation.

One of my own clients, Clifton Eugene Belyeu, was executed
by the State of Texas in 1997. Though I did not attend the execution, I was part of a team of lawyers who represented him. That
execution continues to haunt me, as do all the stories of murder
and violence that I read about and see on the evening news. How
can one not be moved by the obituaries of those killed in the
World Trade Center, newspaper photographs of smiling children
who were later murdered by a stranger or a parent, or television
footage of the bloody aftermath of suicide bombings in Israel?[9]

The execution of a convicted killer whose guilt has been established by a jury is, of course, different in kind from a murderer's
killing of an innocent victim. One is state sanctioned and the
other is not. At an execution, government officials methodically
carry out the act pursuant to legal process, while a murder is per-

petrated by a violent offender, someone who usually has a prior criminal record or history of violence. One of the questions this book asks, however, is whether the death penalty's use does not have more to do with violence (and less to do with crime control) than we've allowed ourselves to believe.

The death penalty, I have found, is an issue about which most people hold deeply felt views, and rightfully so: human life is precious, and anytime someone takes a life the loss is immeasurable. When I talk to people about capital punishment, the first question they usually ask is whether I am for it or against it. After that, I am often asked a question along these lines: Why would a Minnesota lawyer care about capital punishment or bother to get involved in death penalty litigation? It's a fair question. Minnesota is, after all, one of the few states without a death penalty statute, and my home state has witnessed no executions for many decades. Indeed, there are so many problems in the world crying out for solutions—international terrorism, child poverty, homelessness, drug and alcohol abuse, and gun violence, to name just a few—that many people see the fate of convicted killers as inconsequential.

I do not share that view. While capital punishment may never be the most pressing issue in our hectic, day-to-day lives, it merits our attention nevertheless because of what it symbolizes—institutionalized violence. Just as people without cancer or HIV should care about what the government is doing to help find a cure for AIDS and other deadly diseases, we should all pay attention to what our own government is doing in our names. For when a government executes someone, it sends the ill-conceived message that the use of violence against already incarcerated individuals is acceptable. This book, more than anything else, is an attempt to show the deleterious effects of violence and why people should care—in fact, be outraged—that government-sponsored killings, carried out for centuries, are still taking place in this day and age.

Although Minnesota is far away from where executions typically occur, my involvement in this issue has a lot to do with one Minneapolis lawyer—James Volling—and one local organization, Minnesota Advocates for Human Rights, which runs the Death Penalty Defense Project. That project recruits Minnesota lawyers—approximately one hundred so far—to handle postconviction death penalty appeals, mostly in southern states. In such places as Louisiana and Texas there is a dire shortage of attorneys who are willing to handle these unpopular cases, and the Death Penalty Defense Project was set up to help fill that gap.[10]

I first met Jim Volling as a young lawyer at Faegre & Benson, a Minneapolis law firm where I did mostly construction and employment litigation—mechanics' liens, discrimination cases, and the like. It was nothing more than an e-mail message from Jim asking for help on a pro bono matter in Texas that led me to work on my first death penalty case, that of Clifton Belyeu. As a law clerk to the late Chief Justice Warren Burger, Jim Volling saw firsthand the abysmal quality of legal representation that so many criminal defendants receive at their capital trials. While clerking for the nation's highest court, Jim resolved to do something about the inequities he saw. By giving death row inmates access to top-notch lawyers, Jim Volling made good on that promise. It was Jim's example, more than anything else, that put me on the path my life has taken over the last decade.[11]

This book tries to answer the many questions I have asked myself over that time: Do executions make America a safer place to live? What does the future hold for the death penalty? And what drives Americans' lust for it? Are today's executions the byproduct of America's frontier days and the Wild West attitudes that once prevailed in some places? Or is America's ongoing love affair with the death penalty nothing more than a gut reaction to murders, deadly school shootings, and terrorist attacks such as the Oklahoma City bombing? In short, is the death penalty just part of an age-old desire for vengeance that cannot be suppressed?

Just what exactly, at bottom, drives people to kill one another, be it on the streets of Kansas City or Los Angeles, in Pakistan or Tel Aviv, or in an execution chamber in Texas?

Because we live in a society where violence is a major problem, these questions are of utmost importance to ask. Just as critical, of course, are the answers, for America's highly contentious death penalty debate should be informed by facts, not myths or untruths. In my quest for answers, I begin with a story about the place—Texas's death row—where Clifton Belyeu spent much of his life.

ONE

The Manhunt

On Thanksgiving night in 1998, a convicted killer, Martin Gurule, and six other murderers gathered shortly after 8:00 P.M. in
the recreation yard of the maximum-security prison fifteen miles
outside of Huntsville, Texas. Normally confined to their cells for
twenty-three hours a day, these death row inmates had been allowed into the caged-in yard after supper. Relying on special privi-
leges they had earned in a prison work program, the men hatched
a far-fetched escape plan that resembled the plot of a poorly
scripted B movie. When the other inmates returned to their cells,
Gurule and his six fellow convicts disappeared and were left un-
accounted for by the guards.[1]

Having made dummies out of blankets and pillows and put
them on their cell cots to fool the guards, the seven men used a
pilfered hacksaw blade to cut a small hole in an interior fence,
which they climbed through to gain access to the Ellis I Unit's

flat rooftop. There, while waiting for darkness, the men darkened their standard-issue long underwear to avoid detection, using black felt-tip pens and carbon paper from the prison commissary. After waiting more than three hours, the men—still not missed—jumped down from the roof shortly after midnight and dashed across the prison yard toward two chain-link perimeter fences topped with razor wire.[2]

"Just run" was the death row inmates' strategy, as relayed later by Gustavo Garcia, one of the seven, a man facing execution for the shotgun slaying of a store employee during a robbery. As part of the plan, Martin Gurule wore cardboard under his clothes and wrapped magazines around his arms with elastic to protect himself from the fences' sharp metal blades. By the time Gurule reached the top of the second fence, though, the guards had spotted the men, sounded the alarms, and flicked on yellowish perimeter lights.[3]

When the fleeing inmates were seen from two hundred feet away, multiple AR-15 rifle shots rang out from two watchtowers. Six of the inmates, all between the ages of twenty-two and thirty-one, immediately lay down and surrendered. But twenty-nine-year-old Gurule, leaving drops of blood on his way, cleared both fences. He disappeared into the foggy night, becoming the first Texas convict to escape from death row in sixty-four years—a member of Bonnie and Clyde's gang being the last, in 1934.[4]

Gurule, convicted of killing a Corpus Christi restaurant owner during a robbery in which two people were killed, ran past the warden's house and into the 17,000 swampy, wooded acres surrounding the prison. The previously unthinkable was now a reality: a death row inmate was on the loose.[5]

The jailbreak set off a media frenzy and a manhunt involving three helicopters, horse and boat patrols, five hundred searchers, and seventy tracking dogs. By scouring snake-infested woods and creek beds and areas crawling with fire ants and alligators, authorities made an all-out effort to recapture Gurule, who was now, with little food and no drinkable water, among the water moccasins of East Texas's mosquito-laden swamps and bayous. A Texas National Guard helicopter with special equipment capable of detecting heat sources was brought in to find him. "This helicopter can fly over an area, and when it senses a heat source, it can determine the difference between a person or livestock or a rabbit," explained prison spokesman Larry Fitzgerald.[6]

In the days following the escape, prison officials insisted that Gurule remained inside the search perimeter set up around the Huntsville prison. Still, a "wanted" poster with three photos of Gurule, offering a $5,000 reward, was distributed statewide and on the Internet. This prompted several reports of sightings of Gurule throughout the state by nervous citizens. "Somebody saw him eating french fries in a café, or at church on Sunday, or in Dallas with a transvestite," one frustrated prison official told a reporter.[7]

The escape was a public relations nightmare for Texas Governor George W. Bush, who had pushed for a 1995 Texas law to speed up executions by requiring that substantive appeals and habeas petitions be brought at the same time. Eyeing the presidency and having just returned from a trip to the Middle East, Bush was understandably livid about the fugitive's escape. "I'm upset about it," he said, emphasizing that he had asked the Texas Rangers, the state's investigative arm, to find out how it could have happened.[8]

After seven days and seven nights, the huge manhunt came to an abrupt halt. Two off-duty correctional officers who were fishing found Gurule's bloated body at 5:30 P.M. beneath a bridge on Harmon Creek, which feeds into the Trinity River. At first, they thought the figure was a mannequin, but then one of the men, Mark Humphrey, said, "Oh, man, if it's got fingernails, it's not a mannequin." An autopsy showed that Gurule had a shallow, nonlethal bullet wound in his back, but had actually drowned in the creek, the weight of his makeshift cardboard body armor pulling him under the water.[9]

In the end, Gurule got less than a mile away from the prison and probably lasted less than a few hours after his escape. Authorities surmised that Gurule was forced into the rain-swollen, swiftly moving creek by the sound of howling dogs and men on horseback. "I said a prayer for his family," Mark Humphrey said after finding Gurule's body. "I know he had a grandmother, and I feel for her. I feel for the victims, too."10

The botched jailbreak and Gurule's desperate dash into an isolated swamp raised disturbing questions about the level of security at Texas prisons. A full-blown investigation quickly ensued, and just two months after the incident, the warden of the Ellis Unit, Bruce Thaler, was demoted to an administrative job, his two assistant wardens were transferred, and several correctional officers were reprimanded. "We're taking this very seriously," Wayne Scott, the prison system's executive director, said as part of the disciplinary actions. "We're changing the entire management team." The garment-factory work program for death row inmates was canceled, and motion detectors and more razor wire were installed. Gurule's escape was said to be the product of "human error." As one prison board member explained: "We have policies and procedures to prevent this from happening. But when employees are negligent or don't perform duties at all, systems break down."11

Ultimately, the state's death row for all male prisoners was moved from the Ellis Unit to the Terrell Unit outside Livingston, Texas. At Ellis, overcrowding meant two death row inmates per cell; at the Terrell Unit, only one inmate occupies each cell and condemned killers have no physical contact with one another, even in the recreation yard. At the new prison facility, death row prisoners are handcuffed through a small metal slot for any movement from their cells, including showers.12

Although the relocation of death row came after Gurule's escape, Texas officials denied his escape was responsible for the move. "The primary reason we transferred death row from Ellis to Terrell was for capacity," said institutional division director Gary Johnson. "We made a decision that for as long as we could, we wanted death row located at one unit, and that was not going to be possible anymore at Ellis. It really didn't have anything to do with the fact that we had an escape from death row." "You've got to be realistic," added Officer Reginald Bradford, a fifteen-year death row veteran. "Even if the guy hadn't gone over the fence, we were going to have to do something sooner or later, anyway. We were running out of room." In spite of its notoriety, none of the 119 officers who manned Ellis's death row put in for a transfer to the Terrell unit, where the condemned inmates displaced some five hundred administrative segregation inmates who got transferred to new, high-security facilities.[13]

Americans were rightfully appalled by Gurule's escape, particularly as it was not the only escape from death row in recent times. In 1984, an astonishing total of six men—Linwood Briley, James Briley, Earl Clanton, Willie Leroy Jones, Derick Peterson, and Lem Tuggle—escaped from Virginia's Mecklenburg Correctional Center. After taking and locking up hostages, the Mecklenburg Six took control of the cell block, put on guards' uniforms, and fabricated a bomb threat. In the confusion that followed, the men—with Linwood Briley facing an imminent execution date—exited the death house and drove an old white van out of the prison gates. Just hours later, Virginia Governor Chuck Robb would find himself turning to the state's Army and Air National Guard for help in capturing the fugitives.[14]

The scene was little different from the chaos that followed Martin Gurule's escape. After roadblocks were set up and hundreds of law enforcement officers were brought in to assist with the search, teams of bloodhounds and helicopters with infrared equipment scoured the area. Two of the fugitives, Earl Clanton and Derick Peterson, were captured by a SWAT team without incident in a laundromat after they had spent nineteen hours on the run. The other four fugitives had split off and would not be captured so quickly. (Tragically, one local resident, seeing the helicopters and a roadblock near his house and sensing danger, left a loaded pistol on his nightstand. Two days later, his nine-year-old son picked up the gun and, thinking it unloaded, accidentally shot a three-year-old neighbor girl between the eyes.)[15]

After dropping off the Briley brothers in Philadelphia, Lem Tuggle and Leroy Jones, desperate for money, headed for Canada, camping along the way. Tuggle robbed a souvenir shop owner at knifepoint but was pulled over and surrendered peacefully after ten days at large. "I think you'll find I'm wanted pretty bad by the people back in Virginia," he said, raising his hands as a policeman approached him, gun drawn. A convicted rapist and murderer, Tuggle had been sentenced to die for killing a woman in 1983 after having been paroled just months earlier from a 1971 murder sentence. Just ten miles from the Canadian border, Leroy Jones, convicted of murdering an elderly couple, made a collect call to his mother, who convinced him to turn himself in. An unarmed Jones, who telephoned the Vermont State Police, gave himself up by waiting in the middle of a road.[16]

The Briley brothers, who had committed at least eleven murders between them, were not captured until nineteen days after their escape. The two worked quietly as watchmen and handymen at Dan's Custom Car Factory in Philadelphia but were arrested after Lem Tuggle tipped off authorities as to the Briley brothers' whereabouts. On a hot evening in June, as the Briley brothers sat eating barbecued chicken, police officers surrounded the garage, yelling, "Freeze! FBI!" Armed with shotguns, M-16s, and rifles, the law enforcement officers left the brothers with no choice. They were led off in handcuffs without resistance. Robert Landon, the director of Virginia's prison system, called what led to the mass escape "a complete breakdown" in prison rules by the guards.[17]

These two escape attempts and the ensuing manhunts lead to a host of questions: Just what exactly were these men thinking when they sprinted toward the razor-wire fences or, in the case of the Mecklenburg Six, rode a van out of the prison gate? Did these men really believe that they could, against all odds, escape from maximum-security prisons and not get caught or killed in the process? Even though the chances of successful escapes approached nil, there these men were, making mad dashes from the prisons where they were confined.

The men in Texas, running toward barbed wire fences amid gunfire, made a particularly pathetic sight. These hardened criminals were dressed in long underwear and white prison jump suits dyed with black Magic Markers. A stranger sight, except perhaps in a surrealistic film like *O Brother, Where Art Thou?*, is hard to imagine.[18]

For us to comprehend the men's mindset, one fact cannot be overlooked: each of the men was living under a sentence of death. They had little to lose, as they were going to die in the end anyway. "I don't regret trying to escape," Gustavo Garcia told the Associated Press after taking part in the failed escape attempt. "It was worth the try." When asked to compare the risky escape attempt with the prospect of lethal injection, Garcia replied, "Facing execution is scarier."[19]

On that Thanksgiving night in Texas, it was actually state prison officials who had the most cause for concern. They had neglected to put extra rolls of razor wire—at a cost of a few dollars per square foot—between the two perimeter fences, making the escape possible. Not only did the lax security put lives at risk, but in the immediate aftermath of Gurule's escape, Texas officials feared that if Gurule made it to Mexico they might never get him back. As a San Antonio defense lawyer, Gerald Goldstein, explained, "Mexico, like most civilized nations in the world, does not have a death penalty. Their extradition treaty with the United States is clear; they will not extradite, meaning forcibly return, a person who is faced with that penalty."[20]

Most people, like me, just read about Martin Gurule's escape and the escape of the Mecklenburg Six. They did not personally know Martin Gurule or any of the six Virginia death row escapees, whom they were convicted of killing, or the details of these inmates' lives. The names of the Mecklenburg Six and Martin Gurule became widely known only because of their reckless, foolhardy jailbreaks and the public safety issues created by them. Had the Mecklenburg Six not escaped from death row, their executions would have gone forward with little notice. And had Martin Gurule simply stayed put, his lethal injection in Texas would have drawn far less media exposure than that generated by his short-lived escape.

In this day and age, a typical execution attracts very little media attention, particularly outside the state in which the crime occurred. Our world faces so many threats and pressing problems that a convicted killer's demise is easy to overlook. Clifton Belyeu's execution was the thirteenth in a long list of state-sanctioned killings in Texas in 1997. It was reported without a byline and warranted only three sentences in the *New York Times*.[21]

Indeed, newspapers like the *Houston Chronicle* have stopped sending reporters to cover Texas executions at all, relying instead on brief wire-service reports. Unless an execution involves a notorious killer like Timothy McVeigh or, perhaps, a foreign national, television stations have little or no interest and newspapers often cover executions in two-line blurbs in places like the *Washington Post*'s "Addenda" section.[22]

What I have come to believe in the wake of Clifton Belyeu's execution is that Americans continue to execute people because they think about the death penalty, if at all, in only the most abstract way. A cold-blooded killer or a child molester took a life; the public, which never sees executions, wants swift retribution—an eye for an eye, a tooth for a tooth—and many politicians and judges are all too willing to oblige those desires. Television cameras are forbidden at executions, and because they are conducted in an almost anonymous fashion, the American people never see executions for what they are: violent acts.[23]

Paradoxically, while CNN and the major television networks regularly cover murders and war crimes, no American execution has ever been shown on television, allowing Americans to avert their eyes from the state's ultimate sanction. They see grisly images of decaying corpses and mass graves in Kosovo, yet they are deemed unfit by state bureaucrats and lawmakers to watch executioners at work in their own country. This reality has led to apathy, which in turn has led to more and more executions, all of which go unwatched by ordinary Americans.[24]

While television coverage of lethal injections, which have almost totally replaced other, more gruesome forms of execution, might not shock or disturb everyone, exposing the clinical way in which criminals are executed would cause many people to rethink their views. At the very least, such news reports would make executions tangible events involving real people: people who oversee executions and those whose lives are taken by them.[25]

Just how many more executions, I wonder, will Americans allow to take place before they are outlawed? At last count, Watt Espy, the director of the Capital Punishment Research Project in Alabama, has documented that over 19,000 people have been executed from colonial times to the present in what is now the United States. It is a staggering number, but one, I am certain, that is sure to grow in the coming years. States like Texas continue to execute people, and George W. Bush, the man who oversaw a record number of executions in his home state, now sits in the White House.[26]

Already, participants in Martin Gurule's failed Thanksgiving night jailbreak have been executed. In May 2000, James Edward Clayton was executed in Huntsville, Texas, for the murder of an elementary schoolteacher. "He lived too long and died too easy," the schoolteacher's stepfather said after watching the execution of one of the seven men who tried to escape. "I don't think it's painful enough," added the murder victim's still grief-ridden brother. Clayton, a former ROTC member, went to his death having admired his father for killing his neighbor's dog. The convicted murderer once told acquaintances that he could kill a man with an ice pick and said he wanted to be in the army so he would have "a license to kill."[27]

Just as American executions continue, so too do security problems at Texas's fifty-eight prisons, which average about fifteen escapes a year. One of those escapes—a high-profile prison break involving a large group of prisoners—caught my eye when I read about it in my local newspaper. That escape involved no death row inmates, but the escaped convicts were just as dangerous as many of the men on Texas's death row.[28]

Seven felons—serving time for crimes such as kidnapping, robbery, sexual assault, and murder—escaped in December 2000 from a maximum-security prison near Kenedy, Texas, about sixty miles southeast of San Antonio. Six of them worked together in a maintenance shop and overpowered nine maintenance supervisors and four guards before stealing some civilian clothes. The inmates then commandeered .357 Magnum pistols and escaped in a state-owned truck, later found in a Wal-Mart parking lot. The well-armed men were soon wanted in the shooting death of twenty-nine-year-old police officer Aubrey Hawkins. On Christmas Eve, Hawkins was shot eleven times and run over twice while investigating the robbery of a Dallas-area store from which twenty-five weapons were stolen. One of the fugitives committed suicide inside a motor home, but after forty-two days at large, the others were finally captured in Colorado. In an eighty-three-page report, Texas officials again blamed guards for the escape. George Rivas, the ringleader of the prison breakout, was sentenced to death after pleading guilty to Aubrey Hawkins's slaying and asking the jury to give him the death penalty. "I don't want to just exist anymore like an animal in prison," Rivas told jurors.[29]

In another mishap at a Texas prison, death row inmates Ponchai Wilkerson and Howard Guidry—both participants in the failed 1998 Thanksgiving night escape attempt—took fifty-seven-year-old prison guard Jeanette Bledsoe hostage for thirteen hours in February 2000. Wilkerson had been sentenced to death for robbing and shooting a jewelry store owner and was facing a March execution date. Despite tightened security measures implemented after Gurule's escape, Wilkerson got his hands on a rod that had been sharpened to a point, jimmied the lock to his cell, and seized Bledsoe. Guidry, convicted of killing a woman in a murder-for-hire scheme, had a tool that guards use to open food slots on the cell doors. The two men, demanding a moratorium on executions and protesting the living conditions in their six-by-nine-foot cells, eventually surrendered without injuring Bledsoe, but only after being allowed to meet with a group of Houston capital punishment opponents. Just moments before his execution in March 2000, Wilkerson mysteriously spit out a key while strapped to the gurney.[30]

Of course, any prison, in Texas or elsewhere, can be a dangerous place to be. Prisons are where we lock up murderers, rapists, and other violent offenders, and felons often commit acts of violence more than once. In America, however, it is, ironically, those who work the streets—taxicab drivers and police officers—who die more often from homicide than the men and women who guard America's prisoners. In spite of the concentration of violent offenders in prisons, the rate of inmate-on-inmate homicides in state prisons nationwide—5.6 homicides per 100,000 inmates—is actually lower than the homicide rate for the U.S. population as a whole. The annual rate of inmate–on–correctional staff homicides is even lower still, at 1.5 staff homicides per 1,000,000 inmates. OSHA fatality statistics show that fishers, loggers, and construction workers, not correctional officers, top the list of workers with the highest rates of fatal injuries.[31]

While assaults within Texas's 148,000-inmate system are infrequent, serious ones do occur on death row and at other prison facilities statewide. Forty-eight assaults with weapons, for example, were reported throughout Texas prisons in 1999; in December of that year, one correctional officer, Danny Nagle, was killed in the line of duty after being stabbed at the McConnell Unit near Beeville. His death, for which prosecutors brought capital murder charges, was the first of a Texas prison guard in seventeen years.

Just a month earlier, Nagle had stood up at a rally in Austin, Texas, and warned that "someone would have to die" before state officials did anything to address understaffed prisons and underpaid and overworked guards.[32]

It is the isolation of death row that drives many mentally disturbed inmates to even greater heights of madness. In June 2000, for instance, a Hispanic death row inmate, Juan Soria, viciously attacked a seventy-eight-year-old volunteer chaplain, nearly severing his right arm. Facing an execution date the next month for a 1985 robbery-slaying in Fort Worth, Soria pulled the chaplain's arm into the cell up to the elbow, then took out two razor blades and repeatedly slashed the chaplain's arm, breaking it in the process. Soria was a teenager and a ninth-grade dropout when he committed his crime, the murder of Allen Bolden, a seventeen-year-old lifeguard. A migrant worker, Soria had an erratic job history and had been expelled from the family home just before the murder. In 1994, the Texas Court of Criminal Appeals initially ordered that his death sentence be set aside; on the State's motion for a rehearing, however, it was reinstated by that same court in 1996. Soria's vicious attack came just three months after a federal appellate court denied Soria's request to hear his case.[33]

Prison overcrowding and the low morale of prison guards almost certainly account for many of the problems at Texas prisons. "We think it's at a crisis stage," said Brian Olsen, deputy director of the American Federation of State, County, and Municipal Employees, a union representing roughly 4,000 of the state's 23,500 corrections officers. Salaries for prison guards start at $18,000 a year and are capped at $28,000, putting Texas forty-third in the nation in terms of pay for correctional employees. "It's a tough situation, I'm not denying that," says Mac Stringfellow, who oversees the state's prison system. "I think we're doing the best we can with what we've got." The low pay has contributed to a staff shortage of 2,500 guards, and attrition rates show that one in five corrections officers quit in 2000. The Connally unit near Kenedy, Texas, was understaffed by twenty-two officers when the seven inmates broke out of that prison, and only after eighteen months of protests did George W. Bush, near the end of his term as governor, take administrative steps to raise guards' salaries by one thousand dollars.[34]

Looking back, just what conclusions can be drawn from the lapses of security at Texas prisons? That incarcerated offenders cannot be trusted? That is self-evident. Indeed, the very reason we put violent criminals behind bars is to prevent future acts of violence. That understaffed prisons are dangerous places to work? Of course. While safety precautions can and must be taken, that conclusion is inescapable. Prison guards themselves recognize the inherent risks of their chosen profession and accept them. As one Texas corrections employee put it, "All of us who work in prisons know that there's always a chance of assault, that there's always a chance of being taken hostage. It's certainly an event that we all know is possible."[35]

What about this lesson from the escapes and assaults at Texas prisons: that no institution run by people is perfect or ever will be. If prison guards make mistakes and are sometimes negligent in the performance of their duties, what about prosecutors, defense lawyers, judges, and juries? Do they make mistakes? If so, what consequences do those mistakes carry, not only for criminal defendants but also for society as a whole? The realization that any system designed and operated by human beings is fallible should give anyone pause, especially where the issue of capital punishment is under consideration. Has racial bias ever affected a charging decision or a jury's verdict, perhaps in a death penalty case? Certainly. Has an innocent man ever been sent to death row? Without question. So long as the criminal justice system is run by people, as it must be, serious errors, sometimes even fatal ones, will be made.

TWO

In Cold Blood

America's death penalty: it has always been an enigma for me. While executions are still carried out in developing countries such as Bangladesh, Indonesia, and North Korea, the United States and Japan stand virtually alone among industrialized nations in using capital punishment. Canada, Mexico, and all European countries have abolished it, and since 1990 over 30 nations have done away with the death penalty for all crimes. In total, 111 countries no longer authorize death sentences, permit them only in wartime, or have seen no executions for ten years or more. With 74 countries or sovereign territories having abolished the death penalty for all crimes, only 84 countries now retain the death penalty, though fewer still, in practice, actually use executions. In 2001, 5,265 people were sentenced to die in 69 countries, but just a small fraction of the world's nations, 31 countries, were responsible for the 3,048 known executions worldwide that year.[1]

Because America occupies such a prominent role in world affairs, it is not surprising that America's use of the death penalty, especially in circumstances outlawed almost universally elsewhere, has not gone unnoticed by the world community. While European human rights organizations such as the Council of Europe and Hands Off Cain have called for a moratorium on America's death penalty, Americans, in the last decade, have executed more juvenile offenders than any other country. Since 1990, just seven nations—Congo, Iran, Nigeria, Pakistan, Saudi Arabia, Yemen, and the United States—have executed prisoners who were under eighteen years of age at the time of their crimes. And the total number of American executions has reached levels not seen in many years. In 1997, seventy-four people were executed in the United States, the highest total in forty-two years, and that number climbed even higher, to ninety-eight, in 1999.[2]

While the pace of American executions has slowed more recently, it remains the case that, in executing people, we stand largely in the company of a handful of totalitarian regimes—the likes of China, Iran, and Iraq, nations we frequently condemn as violators of human rights. According to Amnesty International, China, Iran, Saudi Arabia, and the United States—a tiny fraction of the world's countries—carry out roughly 90 percent of the world's executions. In 2001, at least 2,468 people are known to have been executed in China; at least 139 executions took place in Iran; 79 executions were reported in Saudi Arabia; and 66 people were executed in the United States. Chinese executions are carried out by pistol shots to the back of the head, with over 18,000 people in China having been executed since 1990 for such crimes as murder, bribery, embezzlement, drug trafficking, and tax evasion. Afghanistan's Taliban regime executed two women convicted of prostitution in early 2001, and Saudi Arabia not only executes people but also continues to cut off limbs as a form of punishment.[3]

As far as I can tell, vengeance is, and always has been, the main driving force behind executions. This certainly seems to have been the case for serial and mass murderers like John Wayne Gacy and Timothy McVeigh, and it is true for lower-profile cases too. "Fry 'em" is a phrase I often hear, and polling shows that "a life for a life" is the most popular justification given for capital punishment. This eye-for-an-eye, life-for-a-life mentality certainly comports with my own experience in watching Texas's criminal justice system operate.[4]

In the 1990s, I worked on two death penalty cases being handled by Sandra Babcock, a Harvard-educated lawyer then at the now-defunct Texas Resource Center, a defender organization that represented death row inmates. Both cases, not surprisingly, involved brutal crimes. Joseph Faulder was convicted of murdering an elderly widow, and Wayne East was found guilty of slaying seventy-seven-year-old artist Mary Eula Sears during a burglary of her home in Abilene, Texas. What I was shocked to learn was that both men had been prosecuted at their criminal trials by private prosecutors hired and paid for by the murder victims' families.

In Faulder's case, two private attorneys were paid roughly $90,000 to prosecute him. A public prosecutor was assigned to work on the case, but his participation was limited to jury selection, where he questioned a few prospective jurors, and to reading into the record the testimony of a deceased hearsay declarant. During trial, the public prosecutor examined no witnesses and made no objections or arguments to the jury. He even took one afternoon off during the trial to play golf.

Though I had never heard of such a thing, the law and the courts allowed the victims' families to hire and pay for the private prosecutors even though this practice creates obvious conflicts of interest. In the end, Faulder was executed in 1999 after spending over twenty years on death row, though Wayne East got his death sentence vacated in 1997 because the prosecution failed to disclose the criminal history of a key prosecution witness. That witness, who gave damaging testimony against East, had been found mentally incompetent to stand trial on an earlier, undisclosed burglary charge and had a history of hallucinations.[5]

It is fair to say, I think, that many facts about America's death penalty, like the use of private prosecutors, are never brought to light. Although countries like China and Guatemala often conduct public executions—Afghanistan and Rwanda have executed people in sports stadiums—the United States prefers to keep its own executions out of the public eye. Thus, while film footage of tank and mortar fire and bombings and terrorist attacks are shown regularly on television, TV news cameras are strictly forbidden in execution chambers. Before Timothy McVeigh's execution, U.S. Attorney General John Ashcroft announced that it would be watched by only a few official witnesses in the Terre Haute, Indiana, federal execution center and by 232 survivors and victims' families in Oklahoma City. The closed-circuit images, he said, would be encrypted and not recorded, so as to leave no permanent record of the event.[6]

If the rest of the civilized world—even Russia and South Africa no longer execute criminals—finds the death penalty so barbaric, why do Americans still execute people in record numbers? Texas alone has over 450 men and women on death row, and in just the four-year period from 1998 to 2001, 317 inmates were put to death in American prisons. While it has produced some of the world's greatest champions of human rights, people such as Martin Luther King, Jr., and Eleanor Roosevelt, the United States continues to execute prisoners month after month even as the international community moves away from executions. "The forfeiture of life is too absolute, too irreversible, for one human being to inflict it on another, even when backed by legal process," United Nations Secretary General Kofi Annan has said, noting his belief "that future generations throughout the world will come to agree."[7]

What is at work here? Do Americans truly believe that the death penalty deters crime better than life imprisonment without the possibility of parole? Or, do we just have a love affair or infatuation with violence?

Americans used to believe that executions deterred murderers, even if the real reason they favored capital punishment was retribution. A 1991 poll, for example, found that over half of those polled believed that the death penalty deterred crime, though only 13 percent cited deterrence as the basis for their support. But the public's views have changed. By 1997, 52 percent of survey respondents—a majority—said the death penalty was not a deterrent. Criminologists and the vast majority of police chiefs and county sheriffs agree. American police chiefs and sheriffs rank the death penalty last among seven potential ways to reduce crime, and 87 percent of criminologists and 57 percent of police chiefs find it totally or largely accurate to say that "debates about the death penalty distract Congress and state legislatures from focusing on real solutions to crime problems."[8]

As a lawyer who has represented death row inmates, I have seen America's death penalty machinery up close. After reading hundreds of death penalty cases, the one thing that becomes clear is that killers are deranged or mentally disturbed when they commit their crimes, totally lack judgment, and show an utter disregard for societal values. How could this not be the case, actually? Gang members, Mafia hit men, or others may kill with premeditation or even, at times, for money, but is there really any doubt but that those who do kill lack the moral compass that guides the behavior of the rest of us? Clearly, anyone who murders another cannot possibly be thinking clearly.

That someone demented enough to kill someone would, before doing so, rationally weigh and consider what the punishment might be seems, at least in the typical case, unlikely at best. What is in the mind of killers when they shoot or stab someone is rage, or perhaps delusions, confusion, or greed, not intelligence or a rational thought process at work. Because murderers operate outside the accepted norms of human behavior and other members of society should be free to live their lives without fear, public safety requires that those who kill be put in maximum-security prisons.

I have never actually witnessed an execution, but I was watching my digital clock in Minneapolis, Minnesota, when Texas executed Clifton Belyeu, the thirty-eight-year-old man I helped represent. Belyeu was a seventh-grade dropout, and he had a violent past and criminal record long before his conviction for murder. He had worked off and on as a dishwasher, a painter, and a drywaller, and before landing on death row, he had had trouble making his car payments and paying his rent.[9]

Once on death row, Clifton Belyeu, to be sure, had a lot of time—much of it spent in isolation—to painfully consider his past behavior. I really doubt, however, that Clifton Belyeu, before committing a crime, ever rationally considered the legal consequences of his actions. If he had, he would not have gotten into trouble with the law or generated a rap sheet in the first place.

An execution does not stop future acts of violence; it merely creates violence. After eating his last meal—a cheeseburger, french fries, and a Coke—Clifton Belyeu soberly fashioned his last words, "God help you, because what you're doing here today and what's in your hearts here today makes you no better than any man or woman on death row across this country." He then died by lethal injection at 6:21 P.M. at the Huntsville prison on May 16, 1997. Belyeu's fate was to die at the hands of the state, just as scores of other condemned inmates—in Texas and elsewhere—will soon die on a state-owned gurney.[10]

I do not dispute that Clifton Belyeu himself was plenty deserving of punishment. The crime that landed him on death row was a robbery committed in West, Texas, a town fifteen miles north of Waco, on December 10, 1985, with an accomplice, Ernest Moore. The robbery netted $15,000 worth of jewelry, money, and guns and ended in the brutal killing of Melody Bolton, a thirty-six-year-old mother of two. Gerald Bolton, her husband, had dropped off their kids at school and was working at his Chevrolet dealership at the time of the murder.[11]

Belyeu and Moore took Mrs. Bolton hostage as she was leaving her home to go to church to make angel costumes for Christmas programs, and the presence of a swing set and toys at the crime scene made clear that she was the mother of small children.

Bolton's autopsy showed that she died of a shotgun blast to the head that nearly decapitated her and multiple stab wounds to her back. Her hands were tied behind her when her husband found her body on their bed.[12]

A search of Belyeu's trailer home, where he lived with his wife and their four children, produced a sawed-off shotgun barrel and stock, muddy white high-top tennis shoes, and a set of keys to a Ford pickup truck that matched the description of one seen in the Boltons' driveway. In the red-and-white truck that Belyeu and Moore had been seen in on the day of the murder, authorities found a bloody buck knife and five shotgun shells. A pine jewelry box identified as Bolton's, more shotgun shells, and a sawed-off shotgun—with brain fragments and blood splatters all over it—were recovered later from a field, as were Gerald Bolton's missing guns, a 30.06 deer rifle, an 1100 Remington, and a 12-gauge shotgun.[13]

In exchange for a "life" sentence, Ernest Moore pled guilty to murdering Mrs. Bolton. Yet, at Belyeu's trial, the prosecution—which told jurors that Belyeu and Moore were "partners in crime"—sought the death penalty for Belyeu alone. The prosecutor told jurors that Belyeu should be put to death regardless of his role in the crime. "Whether Ernest Moore pulled the trigger, whether Clifton Belyeu pulled the trigger makes no difference," the state's attorney argued. Because Texas law makes no provision for true life-without-parole sentences, Moore is eligible for parole as early as December 11, 2005.[14]

The Texas Court of Criminal Appeals concluded that the prosecution's evidence at Clifton Belyeu's trial "revealed a cold-blooded execution and robbery dually carried out" by Belyeu and Moore. While "blood spatters" on Belyeu's clothing "were more consistent with him being the triggerman," the court ruled, "that evidence, although persuasive, was not conclusive." That appellate court found that the evidence, "albeit circumstantial," was sufficient to sustain Belyeu's conviction, though it emphasized that there was "one victim but two perpetrators" and "no witness to testify who actually executed the victim." Belyeu and Moore had stopped at a house to look at a Corvette for sale before the crime was committed, but witnesses could not remember all the details of what they had seen. Belyeu was wearing jeans and a western shirt and Moore was wearing jeans and a white T-shirt, witnesses recalled, but they could not recall which man was wearing boots and which man had on high-top tennis shoes.[15]

A crucial state witness at Belyeu's trial was thus "blood splatter" expert Sergeant Rod Englert, who testified that the blood splatters on Belyeu's blue jeans were consistent with the blood splatter pattern found on the walls of the Boltons' master bedroom. Sergeant Englert gave the same testimony with respect to a denim jacket and testified further that the blood spatters on Belyeu's jeans—as opposed to those on Moore's jeans—were consistent with the blood splatters found on the denim jacket. Englert offered this damaging expert opinion—the only evidence tending to prove that Belyeu was the triggerman—even though there was an insufficient quantity of blood on the jacket and Belyeu's blue jeans to type it, whereas the Type A blood detected on Moore's jeans matched the deceased's blood type.[16]

Having retained no forensic expert of their own, Belyeu's trial attorneys—one of whom expressed the view that "there is no great deal of magic" to blood spatter evidence—couldn't effectively cross-examine Sergeant Englert or impeach his testimony. As a result, Englert's speculative opinions, couched as "scientific" proof that Belyeu was the shooter, went largely unrebutted.[17]

The trial judge's failure to instruct the jury at the penalty phase of Belyeu's trial that a legal doctrine called the "law of the parties" did not apply also may have affected the jury's deliberations. At the trial's guilt/innocence phase, the jury properly received a law of the parties instruction that authorized Belyeu's conviction if the jury found he "acted either alone or as a party" with Ernest Moore "in the commission of the alleged offense." The jury charge at the trial's penalty phase, however, contained no instruction that the law of the parties doctrine could not be considered at that stage. The trial court's failure to instruct the jury that it could not, in assessing Belyeu's punishment, consider Moore's conduct (as the law permitted it to do in guilt/innocence deliberations), led to a sharply worded dissent on the appeal of Belyeu's death sentence, which the Texas Court of Criminal Appeals let stand despite the error.[18]

These, of course, are moot points because Clifton Belyeu is no longer alive. I mention them only because murder cases, even those involving execution-style killings, often have evidentiary disputes that can never be conclusively resolved, at least not to a 100 percent certainty. Gray areas exist in many criminal prosecutions because videotapes of the crime are available in only the most unusual of cases.

I was not present when Melody Bolton was killed, so I will never know what transpired in her house. I do not know if Clifton Belyeu shot or stabbed her, did both, perhaps, or merely stood by as Ernest Moore killed her. I do know one thing: Clifton Belyeu was clearly capable of violence and certainly culpable for his role in the robbery that led to Melody Bolton's death by virtue of his presence—as found by the jury—at the crime scene.

In fact, when Clifton Belyeu was not incarcerated, he was often a menace to society, especially when he got loaded up on drugs and alcohol. He had served time in prison in 1979 for robbery, stolen property on at least two other occasions, and frequently beat his wife, Donna, giving her black eyes and once inflicting injuries so severe that she could barely walk.[19]

His girlfriend Shirley suffered similar abuse, getting hit and kicked on a regular basis, and Belyeu once attempted to strangle her while she slept. On one occasion, Belyeu hung Shirley's screaming two-year-old daughter by the hair from the second floor of a house. When Shirley grabbed for the child, he released her, and Shirley caught the child only "by the hands of God." In another instance, while on a long drive Belyeu ripped the head off Shirley's pet parakeet, threw the bird's body from the truck, and made her finish the trip with the bird's head in her lap.[20]

These incidents and the chilling facts of Mrs. Bolton's murder are revolting in the extreme. Once the jury found that Clifton Belyeu was at Mrs. Bolton's house when she was murdered, he should have been sent to prison for the rest of his natural life. The death penalty, however, solves nothing; it only brings the rest of us down into the gutter with the perpetrators of violence. Belyeu's execution did not bring back Melody Bolton; it merely compounded a crime by inflicting needless pain on—and stigmatizing—Belyeu's own family members. Just imagine the task of telling a convicted killer's already grief-stricken mother that the state is about to take her own son's life, a killing everyone knows could be avoided by merely incarcerating the offender for life.[21]

In the end, a killer's execution brings no closure to a murder victim's family, as Coretta Scott King and members of Murder Victims' Families for Reconciliation, an anti–death penalty group that helps rebuild shattered lives, can readily attest; it only teaches people the false lesson that violence works. The widow of Dr. Martin Luther King, Jr., following in the footsteps of her slain husband, refuses to accept that killers deserve to die. It would "perpetuate the tragic cycle of violence that feeds itself," she says, merely doing a "disservice" to everything her husband "lived for and believed." As the founder of Murder Victims' Families for Reconciliation aptly asks, "How can we stand as murder victims, in our pain and sorrow, and give it to someone else's family as well?" "We can't stop all violence," one of the organization's brochures says, "but we can work to stop the violence carried out by a government that kills in our names."[22]

Clifton Belyeu himself learned early in life about violence and how to inflict it. He was one of eight children raised by his mother with welfare money after his abusive father went to prison for raping one of Belyeu's sisters.[23]

And Belyeu is hardly alone. The parade of horrors that death row inmates suffered as children is as endless as it is unimaginable to those of us who grew up in nonviolent households. As kids, future death row inhabitants were assaulted with hammers, screwdrivers, and tree limbs, or coat hangers, broomsticks, or belts. They were sometimes beaten unconscious or locked out of the house—naked—or in a closet for hours or days at a time.[24]

Robert Anthony Carter, a black man executed in Texas in 1998, grew up in a Houston housing project and was thrashed by his mother and stepfather with wooden sticks and electric cords. He was struck on the head with a brick at age five; at age ten, he was hit so hard against his skull with a baseball bat that the bat broke; and on another occasion, his mother smashed a dinner plate over his head. When a child is tied up in cotton sacks and hung from garage rafters and whipped with an extension cord or hog-tied and tethered to a hook with a piece of leather, what kind of adult does one really expect will be produced?[25]

John Paul Penry, a Texas inmate thrice sentenced to die, now in his mid-forties, has an IQ of 56. Penry was sent to death row for the brutal 1979 rape and murder of Pamela Carpenter, a twenty-two-year-old woman who sang in her church choir whom Penry repeatedly stabbed with a scissors. As a child, Penry was diagnosed as suffering from organic brain damage, and Penry's mother, institutionalized for nearly a year after her son's birth, constantly beat and humiliated him. She burned him with cigarette butts and in a scalding bath, deprived him of food and water for long periods, and forced him to eat his own feces and drink his own urine out of the toilet. "We were all abused, but he was abused the worst," one of Penry's sisters said. "She would beat him with anything in sight." In an interview, Penry's sister vividly described their mother's treatment of him. "She would threaten to gouge his eyeballs out with her long fingernails. She would threaten to cut off his private parts with a butcher knife." At age twelve, Penry was put in the Mexia State School for the Mentally Retarded, where staff members found many scars on Penry's head when they gave him a haircut upon his arrival. "They were from cuts made by a large belt buckle which his mother used when whipping him," a school report noted. Penry, who believes in

Santa Claus and has the mental age of a six-year-old, passes his time in prison flipping through comic books he cannot read and coloring with crayons.[26]

A recent study found that being abused or neglected as a child increased the likelihood of arrest for such juveniles by 59 percent. While child abuse does not always trigger a life of violent crime, it clearly increases the risk of violent behavior later in life, especially in cases where the abuse is brutal and protracted. A study of fifteen death row inmates found "extraordinary" child abuse in twelve of the cases, with eight being victims of "potentially filicidal assaults"—parental violence that nearly claimed their lives. In one case, a mother shot at her son and threatened him with a knife; in another, a mother burned her son with a hot iron; and in yet another, a father dangled his four-year-old son outside of a car while it sped down the highway. Five of the fifteen had been sexually abused as children—one boy had been raped by a male cousin and forced to fondle his mother's breasts and stimulate her orally—and in twelve of the cases, adults in the child's life had inflicted extreme violence on other adults. Another study of thirty-one murderers found that twenty-six of them had a history of severe and prolonged child abuse.[27]

Not surprisingly, perhaps, death row inmates are often brain damaged or mentally retarded, or have untreated mental illnesses, low IQs, or severe learning disabilities. They have sometimes suffered episodes of torture and often were raised in dire poverty, have taken antipsychotic medications such as Mellaril and Haldol, or been raped or sexually molested in institutions or by a parent, stepparent, cousin, or uncle. Their parents may be drug abusers or live on public assistance and may themselves be mentally ill or have been institutionalized. Approximately 70 percent of death row inmates have been diagnosed with schizophrenia or psychosis. Varnall Weeks, a convicted killer executed in 1995, suffered from paranoid schizophrenia and thought he would come back to life as "a giant flying tortoise that would rule the world."

A Louisiana death row inmate, Michael Owen Perry, convicted of killing five family members and found in a hotel room with the names of each of his victims written on separate television sets, is another diagnosed schizophrenic. He shaved his eyebrows with the intention of getting more oxygen to his brain, and once stated that pop singer Olivia Newton-John, an obsession of his, "is a goddess living under Lake Arthur." Horace Edward Kelly, a California death row inmate, believed he could talk to animals and, at times, believed he was an animal, eating dog food or meals in a tree where he would howl.[28]

Those who commit violent crimes—frequently drunk or on drugs when they do so—have almost always been victimized themselves. Studies have shown, in fact, that childhood physical abuse exponentially increases the odds of interfamilial abuse by the abused individual later in life. Childhood sexual abuse also greatly increases the likelihood of the victims committing such abuse within families and against strangers. A report issued by the U.S. Department of Justice in 2001, which summarized the findings of a long-term study, found that "childhood abuse and neglect increased the odds of future delinquency and adult criminality overall by 29 percent." "This research shows," the report said, "that today's victims of neglect may well be tomorrow's violent offenders." Serial rapists, as children, frequently suffered incest or other forms of sexual abuse, and substance abuse commonly accompanies the use of violence. About four in ten violent crimes involve the use of alcohol.[29]

A couple of Minneapolis colleagues of mine, Greg Merz and Tom Johnson, represent a Texas death row inmate, Peter Miniel, who fits just such a pattern. In 1988, Miniel was convicted of killing a man with a beer mug, a shock absorber, and a small knife after a day spent drinking beer and smoking marijuana. He was the product of an unwanted pregnancy and a miserable childhood, having been adopted by a violent, abusive alcoholic and the sister of his birth mother. His adoptive father, Manuel Miniel, regularly beat Peter with his fists or a belt, and his adoptive mother had bouts of depression so severe that she required hospitalization. Manuel would leave his children alone, either at home or in his car, while he drank at a tavern, and Peter started drinking himself after learning from an angry, belligerent sibling at age twelve that he was adopted. In his teens and early twenties, Peter frequently drank and took drugs until he passed out—once almost freezing to death in the snow—and after dropping out of school at age sixteen he was involved in a series of car accidents that severely cut his face. Each of Peter's siblings attempted suicide at least once, and before arriving on death row, Peter had grown accustomed to the use of violence. He had committed one assault with numchucks and another in which he beat his girlfriend with a wooden spoon and a motorcycle chain.[30]

It is not unusual, when they kill, for violent offenders to be unemployed, despondent, or even suicidal. John Allen Muhammad and John Lee Malvo, the two men apprehended in the D.C.–area sniper case, were living out of a $250 used car when they were arrested. Muhammad, estranged from his second wife and separated from his three children after having abducted them, had been living in a homeless shelter in Washington State. Malvo, left to fend for himself by his mother at age fifteen, befriended Muhammad on the Caribbean island of Antigua and was facing a deportation hearing when the killing spree took place. In a recent murder spree in Japan, a deranged man fatally stabbed eight first- and second-grade students with a kitchen knife and injured fifteen others. It was the deadliest act of violence in that country since a cult's 1995 nerve-gas poisoning of a Tokyo subway killed twelve and injured hundreds. Mamoru Takuma, the divorced man who stabbed the schoolchildren, had been fired from his job as a taxi driver after assaulting a hotel doorman and been charged with spiking the tea of four schoolteachers with tranquilizers. "I just hated everything," Takuma told police after his rampage. "I thought about committing suicide many times," he said, "but I couldn't do it." "I thought maybe I could be sentenced to death," he told authorities.[31]

At the appointed hour for Clifton Belyeu's execution on May 16, 1997—a day I shall not forget—I was sitting hundreds of miles away in Minneapolis feeling utterly powerless, simply waiting for news of the execution by lethal injection. I certainly knew that no last-minute reprieve would come. George W. Bush, the Texas governor, was a well-known death penalty enthusiast who had never even issued a thirty-day stay of execution. The lead lawyer on Belyeu's defense team, Jim Volling, captured everyone's feelings: "We've been through the pardon board process. We've been everywhere we can go: state court, federal court. We have no ability to go anywhere. It's a very helpless feeling."[32]

After Belyeu's last-ditch clemency petition was summarily denied, nothing that Jim or anyone else on the defense team could do or say would make any difference. A fellow lawyer, Tim Rank, and I just settled on observing a minute of silence after getting word of our client's death. It was an awkward moment, for we had done our best to save Clifton Belyeu's life and had failed. I had gone to law school to make a difference, and the loss felt personal, even though I never met Clifton Belyeu face to face and my hundreds of hours of work on the case involved mostly brief writing and legal research.

In thinking back to that excruciating May day, I often wonder whether I should have attended the execution or at least gone to Huntsville, Texas, to become what would have been the fourth protestor that day outside the prison gates. Instead of observing a moment of silence, maybe I should have bought a plane ticket and been there to bear witness or just to hold up a cardboard sign to rail against the taking of human life, which I know to be wrong. Perhaps all of us should have been there, for it is we who let it happen.

THREE

Violence

Throughout history, the world has witnessed countless wars and acts of torture and violence. Dictators such as Julius Caesar and Caligula reigned over the Roman Empire, the Crusaders fought over the Holy Land in a series of wars, and England's King Henry VIII had two of his own wives beheaded for alleged infidelity. The Hundred Years' War pitted France against England, the Peloponnesian War bitterly divided the Greek city-states of Athens and Sparta, and the Trojan War is still remembered today because of Homer's epic the *Iliad*. The last century alone saw the Russo-Japanese War; Mao Tse-tung's and Lenin's revolutions in China and Russia; Stalin's rise to power; the Spanish Civil War; Benito Mussolini's formation of a fascist government in Italy; Adolph Hitler and the Nazis' perpetration of the Holocaust, which killed six million Jews in concentration camps such as Auschwitz and Dachau; the Six-Day War, which pitted Israel against Egypt, Syria, and Jordan; Cambodia's Pol Pot–led Khmer Rouge regime; and genocide and ethnic cleansing in Rwanda and Bosnia.[1]

The casualties of violence are not limited by borders. Africa, Asia, Australia, Europe, and the Americas have all seen the loss of human life, often on a colossal scale. Civil war has torn apart countries such as Sri Lanka and Liberia, death squads have killed priests and nuns in El Salvador, and Americans themselves have fought and died in many battles. The Boston Massacre set the stage for the Revolutionary War and battles at places like Saratoga and Bunker Hill, the Civil War made Gettysburg and Bull Run household names, and World War I and II and the Korean and Vietnam Wars claimed thousands of lives. From Pearl Harbor to D-Day to the My Lai massacre, countless soldiers and civilians have died in wartime. In Argentina's "Dirty War," military commanders ordered the kidnapping and torture of detainees and injected victims with sedatives before shoving their unconscious bodies out of airplanes over the Atlantic Ocean. There have been so many wars that rules governing the treatment of POWs, the Geneva Conventions, were put in place. At the close of the twentieth century, one-third of the world's nations were embroiled in military conflict.[2]

It was when I lived in Kingston, Jamaica, as a college student that I first saw machine guns—a quintessential tool of violence—up close. Just the sight of heavily armed, uniformed men in jeeps holding the weapons made me reflect, as never before, on the dangers and risks posed by violent crime. Despite hearing of brutal machete attacks in Jamaica's prior elections, I had traveled to the Caribbean as part of a university program called Minnesota Studies in International Development; there I found myself living in a house with bars on its windows not far from the most abject poverty I had ever seen. To this day, I can still picture the rows of rusty tin shacks that people live in and an old man with gray hair crouched in a Dumpster looking for discarded scraps of food. In a tiny village in the Blue Mountains, I was struck as much by the lack of chlorinated water and health-care facilities as I was by the lush terrain.

While in Kingston, I had the closest brush of my life with what easily could have become deadly violence. Eager to meet people, I quickly befriended a young man named Trevor who turned out to be a rather talented con artist. After showing me around Jamaica's capital city and taking me to a cricket match, he got me to lend him a couple hundred Jamaican dollars, promising to repay me in a couple of days. After more than two weeks went by and I hadn't been repaid, I decided to write off the money as a lesson learned. Before flying home, though, I discovered that Trevor had other creditors when two guys muscled their way into his house while I was there. One of the men openly brandished a pistol—an old six-shooter, with a revolving, cylindrical chamber—and yelling and swearing ensued as Trevor and the men argued and threatened one another. Luckily, though I felt in grave danger, no one was hurt. The men just took Trevor's girlfriend's hairdressing equipment—representing her livelihood—as a down payment for what he owed them.

Unfortunately, many people, particularly those who live in poverty, have felt the fear I did that day on countless occasions. In poor neighborhoods or impoverished, war-torn countries, drug dealing, gangs, and gun violence or warlords and land mines are often a fact of life. Just imagine what it must be like to live next door to a crack house, to share a roof with an ultraviolent, alcoholic father who always keeps a loaded handgun in the house, or to raise children in a war zone amid falling bombs or the rubble of bullet-ridden homes? Many of the people on death row in places like Jamaica and the United States have grown up in such desolate poverty, where violent crime occurs with some frequency and guns represent power in otherwise powerless communities.

In America alone, thousands of people are killed by guns every year. A 1997 study of twenty-six countries by the Centers for Disease Control found that 86 percent of gun-related deaths of children under age fifteen occurred in the United States. The firearm-related homicide rate for children five to fourteen years old is an astonishing seventeen times higher in the United States than it is in other industrialized nations. In just a typical year, 1995, 35,957 Americans died of gunshot wounds, and every year, almost three times that number are treated in emergency rooms for nonfatal gun injuries. The estimated cost to American society is over $100 billion per year. In all, over three-quarters of a million Americans have been killed since 1960 in firearm-related homicides, suicides, or accidents. The casualties of gun violence range from small children—6,817 aged five to fourteen in one recent ten-year period—to presidents. The gun that Lee Harvey Oswald used to kill John F. Kennedy was purchased through an advertisement in the National Rifle Association's official publication, *American Rifleman*.[3]

Without question, the United States has a disproportionate share of gun-related violence. Seventy-one percent of American homicides are gun related, and firearm injuries are America's seventh leading cause of death. In 1996, handguns were used to murder 9,390 people in the United States, while handgun-related homicides in foreign countries that year were far lower: 213 in Germany, 106 in Canada, 30 in Great Britain, 15 in Japan, and 2 in New Zealand. A one-year study of 36 high- and upper-middle-income countries found that firearm mortality rates ranged from a high of 14.24 deaths per 100,000 people in the United States to a low of 0.05 deaths per 100,000 people in Japan, where less than 1 percent of the public owns guns. The rate of firearm deaths in America was found to be eight times the pooled rate for other high-income countries, and 1.5 times the pooled rate for upper-middle-income countries like Portugal and Greece.[4]

Although hunting and target shooting are lawful activities enjoyed by many law-abiding citizens, the easy access that American kids and felons have to lethal weapons is very disturbing. Deadly school shootings, such as those at Columbine High School and in Jonesboro, Arkansas, show just how accessible guns are in American society, even to teenagers or preteens. When Andrew Golden and Mitchell Johnson, aged eleven and thirteen, pulled a fire alarm at their school in Jonesboro in 1998, then opened fire as children and teachers filed out of the building, whatever innocence Americans had left was shattered. In under four minutes, the two boys—armed with ten guns—killed five and wounded ten others. Schoolchildren lay dead and grieving parents, classmates, and teachers were left to wonder what went so terribly wrong. The sheer number of workplace shootings and rampage killings in America is enough to make anyone wonder how we got to where we are today and what can be done to stop the violence.[5]

A newspaper article in the *New York Times,* headlined "The Biography of a Gun," shows just how much damage a single gun can inflict. That article traces the path of a 9-millimeter semi-automatic handgun, manufactured in 1995 at a factory near John Wayne International Airport in Costa Mesa, California. One of about 200,000 inexpensive handguns made each year at the Bryco Arms plant, the six-inch gun, made partly of plastic, weighs just sixteen ounces. Though it is now locked in a property clerk's office in Brooklyn, the gun was involved in at least thirteen crimes, including two murders and the wounding of at least three other people. The homicide victims were a sixteen-year-old boy sitting atop a mailbox and a forty-eight-year-old father of four. The gun—serial no. 997126—was purchased for ninety dollars by an Ohio wholesaler, sold to a Georgia pawn shop, and then purchased by an associate of a convicted felon before it made its way to New York.[6]

Massive numbers of guns, often stockpiled by hate groups, are in existence. A quarter of adults in America own firearms and at least 190 million guns are in civilian hands. American gun manufacturers produced over 4 million guns in 1995 alone, and between 1978 and 1996 over 20 million more were imported from nations such as Brazil and China for the U.S. civilian market.

Handguns have, at times, accounted for over 60 percent of all gun imports, and the flow of weapons into America, where they frequently change hands, continues. More than 700 firearm importers are licensed by the federal government, and 122 firearms distributors operate in the United States. About 40 percent of gun transfers are largely unregulated, occurring at such places as gun shows and flea markets, and it is a few unscrupulous dealers, who use straw purchasers such as drug addicts and homeless people to fill out federal handgun applications, who supply many of the weapons that end up in police evidence rooms. Just 1.2 percent of the nation's 83,000 licensed dealers supply almost 60 percent of all guns used in crimes.[7]

Though many Americans have never been raped, shot at, or physically assaulted, the concept of violence is familiar to all of us. By age eighteen, the average teenager has seen 200,000 violent acts on television, and almost everyone knows someone whose life has been forever changed by a criminal act. The *American Heritage Dictionary* in my bookcase at home defines "violence" as a physically invasive act: "physical force exerted for the purpose of violating, damaging or abusing." That definition certainly describes fistfights, rapes, and murders, during which people punch, violate, or kill one another; terrorism and war, in which commercial jets, suicide bombers, and tanks and bombs are used to take lives; and state-sanctioned killing, in which inmates are forcibly strapped onto a gurney and executed by lethal injection.[8]

The use of violence can be justified in wartime, to apprehend dangerous criminals, and in cases of self-defense to protect life. World War II, for example, had to be fought to stop Nazi aggression, just as the Taliban's refusal to turn over Osama bin Laden and his henchmen led America to invade Afghanistan to track down heavily armed terrorists. Likewise, when a police officer is shot at in the line of duty, the officer's right to shoot back is clear. Indeed, anytime a law enforcement officer's life is endangered or a person is assaulted, the law of self-defense rightfully empowers a person to protect himself or herself from harm.

When a government already has someone in custody, though, what purpose is served by an execution? Is anything really accomplished by sticking a needle in someone's arm and intentionally killing that person with deadly chemicals? In truth, all an execution does is inject more violence into a society. Because the government should be setting an example for its people, executions are especially counterproductive, particularly where life-without-parole sentences can be used instead to protect the public.

Meticulously planned murders, ruthlessly carried out by sick or deranged murderers, are horrific, there's no denying that. However, are state-sanctioned executions really any different from premeditated killings? What, after all, could be more premeditated than the execution process itself? A legislative body, with its committees and subcommittees, deliberates and passes a death penalty law; a prosecutor asks grand jurors to hand down a capital murder indictment; a twelve-person jury is sworn and decides to impose a death sentence; a series of judges and a pardon board or a governor look at the case and consciously decide to let that sentence stand; and, finally, the executioner carries out the court's orders. It is hard to imagine any form of killing that is more calculated than that.

And history teaches us that, in truth, state-sanctioned killing does nothing to stop violence. A recent study commissioned by the *New York Times* examined FBI data and found that death penalty states' average homicide rates consistently exceed those of non–death penalty states. That study reached the disturbing conclusion that, over the last twenty years, death penalty states' murder rates have been, on a per capita basis, an astonishing 48 percent to 101 percent higher than those in non–death penalty states. Of America's twelve non–death penalty jurisdictions, ten have murder rates below—often far below—the national average. The State of Minnesota, where I live, for instance, abolished capital punishment over ninety years ago, yet has one of the lowest violent crime rates in the country. While the national homicide rate was 6.3 murders per 100,000 people in 1998, Minnesota's murder rate that year was less than half that figure. Active death penalty states such as Texas and Louisiana, on the other hand, regularly have some of the country's highest murder rates.[9]

Of course, many social and economic variables—even weather conditions—can and do affect a state's violent crime rate. Research shows that murder rates are higher in summer months and in poor urban areas with youthful populations, but social scientists—conducting regression and time-series analyses—have repeatedly found no credible evidence that the death penalty deters violent crime more effectively than prison sentences. Comparisons of the homicide rates for neighboring death penalty and abolitionist states certainly lend no support to the deterrence hypothesis, and a recent study of executions and murder rates in Texas found that America's most active death penalty state saw no decrease in homicides as a result of executions. Using data from 1984 through 1997, the authors of that study concluded that "the number of executions was not related to murder rates over the 14-year period that was studied." Control variables that were positively related to homicide rates included the percentage of the population aged eighteen to thirty-four and the months of July and August, when homicide rates tend to be higher.[10]

Indeed, a study done in Oklahoma found no change in the rate of felony murders over the sixty-eight weeks following a well-publicized execution in 1990 but actually observed an increase in the rate of homicides committed by strangers. The mean number of weekly killings involving persons not known to one another was .42 for the pre-execution period examined, compared with an average of .76 for the period after the execution. That same brutalization effect was found in Arizona, where another study observed an increase in several types of homicides in metropolitan areas after that state's first execution in twenty-nine years.[11]

Thus, one thing is clear: the notion that death penalty laws reduce violence is absurd. Indeed, if the death penalty was really thought to deter crime, why wouldn't politicians take steps to better publicize executions so that everyone would see them?

When I think about capital punishment myself, I often think of the madness and absurdity of Clifton Belyeu being strapped down and killed even as his partner-in-crime, Ernest Moore, may some-day be set free. A short story called "The Lottery" also leaps to mind. That story, written by the novelist Shirley Jackson, describes an ancient custom set in modern times; it takes place in an un-identified small town—Anywhere, U.S.A.—where the residents talk of "planting and rain" and "tractors and taxes." Jackson's fic-tional story illustrates realities and principles—arbitrariness, un-fairness, and a lack of mercy and compassion—that come into play when death sentences are meted out by America's judicial system.[12]

The opening line of "The Lottery" describes a vibrant, sunny summer day, with green grass and flowers blossoming every-where. While the story's many characters, all townspeople, act very polite at the outset—the adult characters are referred to as "Mr." and "Mrs."—the story is unsettling. In the beginning, all the reader is told is that the townsfolk are gathering at 10:00 A.M. in the village square between the bank and the post office for a two-hour "lottery" of some undisclosed nature. Children assem-ble first, filling their pockets with stones from a pile of rocks, fol-lowed by the community's three hundred or so men and women, who casually exchange greetings and gossip. As if the lottery was no more extraordinary than a P.T.A. meeting, Shirley Jackson nonchalantly writes that the "lottery was conducted—as were the square dances, the teen-age club, the Halloween program—by Mr. Summers, who had time and energy to devote to civic activi-ties."[13]

A "jovial man" who runs a coal business, Mr. Summers arrives in the town square wearing blue jeans and carrying a mysterious-looking, black wooden box. Right behind him is the postmaster, Mr. Graves, carrying a three-legged stool, which serves as the box's resting place. As the story progresses, two townspeople, Mr. Martin and his oldest son, Baxter, come forward to steady the box on the stool while Mr. Summers stirs up some papers inside it.

"The night before the lottery," the omniscient narrator matter-of-factly reveals, "Mr. Summers and Mr. Graves made up the slips of paper and put them in the box." Before Mr. Summers declares the lottery "open" each year, Mr. Summers is sworn in by the postmaster and lists are drawn up of "heads of households" and members of each family.[14]

Jackson's story gets darker and darker as it goes on. After talking "interminably to Mr. Graves and the Martins," Mr. Summers casually addresses the villagers just as Mrs. Hutchinson, a housewife, comes hurriedly into the square. "Clean forgot what day it was," she tells a Mrs. Delacroix, drying her hands on her apron, "then I looked out the window and the kids was gone, and then I remembered it was the twenty-seventh and came a-running." The good-humored crowd lets her through, and a waiting Mr. Summers says cheerfully, "Thought we were going to have to get on without you, Tessie." Mrs. Hutchinson grins and the crowd laughs before Mr. Summers soberly continues, "Well, now, guess we better get started, get this over with, so's we can go back to work. Anybody ain't here?" The name of Clyde Dunbar, who has a broken leg, is shouted out, prompting Mr. Summers to turn to Mrs. Dunbar, Clyde's spouse, and remind her of the rule, "Wife draws for her husband."[15]

As Mr. Summers clears his throat and consults his list, a hush falls over the crowd. "All ready?" he calls. "Now, I'll read the names—heads of families first—and the men come up and take a paper out of the box. Keep the paper folded in your hand without looking at it until everyone has had a turn." Mr. Summers then begins calling everyone's family names in alphabetical order, "Adams," "Allen," "Anderson," "Bentham," and so on. One by one the family patriarch, or women in the position of Mrs. Dunbar, approach the black box and draw a slip of paper from it. While men throughout the crowd hold the small slips of papers nervously in their hands, Mr. Adams is heard to say to Old Man Warner, "They do say that over in the north village they're talking of giving up the lottery." "Pack of crazy fools," Old Man Warner retorts, "There's always been a lottery. Bad enough to see young Joe Summers up there joking with everybody." Mr. Summers calls the "Warner" name. "Seventy-seventh year I been in the lottery," Old Man Warner says as he maneuvers through the crowd. "Seventy-seventh time."[16]

The drawing of names is followed by a long pause, until Mr. Summers holds his slip of paper in the air. Gradually, as the women begin asking "Who is it?" "Who's got it?" "Is it the Dunbars?" "Is it the Watsons?," all of the slips of paper are unfolded. It isn't long before voices begin saying, "It's Hutchinson. It's Bill," "Bill Hutchinson's got it." Mr. Hutchinson is spotted standing quietly, staring down at the slip of paper in his hand. Just then, Mrs. Hutchinson shouts out to Mr. Summers, "You didn't give him time enough to take any paper he wanted. I saw you. It wasn't fair." The reaction is immediate. "Be a good sport, Tessie," Mrs. Delacroix cries out, and Mrs. Graves exclaims, "All of us took the same chance."

Mr. Summers consults a second list. "Bill," he says, "you draw for the Hutchinson family." Mrs. Hutchinson continues to protest. "It wasn't fair," she calls out again, but Mr. Summers just continues on, asking Mr. Hutchinson, "How many kids, Bill?" "Three," he replies, "There's Bill, Jr., and Nancy, and little Dave. And Tessie and me." Mr. Graves collects the Hutchinson family's five tickets and puts them back in the black box. Again, Mrs. Hutchinson cries foul. "I think we ought to start over," she says, "I tell you it wasn't fair. You didn't give him time enough to choose."[17]

In spite of Mrs. Hutchinson's pleas, Mr. Summers remains unfazed, and readers of Shirley Jackson's story realize that this lottery is one a person seeks *not* to win. "Ready, Bill?" Mr. Summers asks. Mr. Hutchinson, glancing at his wife and children, nods as Mr. Summers continues his instructions, asking for help from the postmaster, Harry Graves: "Remember, take the slips and keep them folded until each person has taken one. Harry, you help little Dave." After all five Hutchinson family members draw a slip from the box, Mr. Summers says, "All right. Open the papers. Harry, you open little Dave's." Mr. Graves opens little Davy's slip first and a sigh of relief goes through the crowd as he holds up a blank slip. Nancy and Bill, Jr., open their slips next and both smile and laugh as they hold their blank slips above their heads. There is a pause before Mr. Hutchinson unfolds his slip—also blank—and Mr. Summers reports what now everyone already knows, "It's Tessie." Mr. Hutchinson forces the slip of paper out of his wife's hand to confirm that it has a black spot on it, the same black spot that Mr. Summers made the night before in heavy pencil in his coal-company office.[18]

The crowd stirs as Mr. Hutchinson holds up the slip of paper, and Mr. Summers calls out, "All right, folks. Let's finish quickly." With that, all the villagers—men, women, and children alike— pick up stones, some so large that they have to be carried with both hands. As Mrs. Hutchinson quickly finds herself in the center of a cleared space, the reader's worst fears are confirmed: the town's annual lottery is about selecting a townsperson to be put to death. As rocks start flying at her, Mrs. Hutchinson desperately holds out her hands in a futile attempt to protect herself. "It isn't fair," she cries as a stone hits her on the side of the head. Old Man Warner quickly moves in on Mrs. Hutchinson and shouts out, "Come on, come on, everyone," and Mr. Adams is seen in the front of the crowd, with Mrs. Graves beside him. "Come on," Mrs. Delacroix, picking up a rock, says to Mrs. Dunbar, "Hurry up."[19]

Jackson's short story, which begins so innocently, ends with Mrs. Hutchinson being stoned to death in the village square. "It isn't fair, it isn't fair," Mrs. Hutchinson screams as the crowd descends upon her. But Mrs. Hutchinson's epiphany—her realization that the lottery ends in nothing more than a senseless act of violence—comes too late. In a few short moments she will be dead, the latest in a long string of victims the town's lottery has claimed.

When it was first published in the *New Yorker* in 1948, the negative response to Jackson's short story was immediate. When Jackson picked up her mail at the post office in the little Vermont town in which she lived, the postmaster would not speak to her. She also got a telling note from a friend: "Heard a man talking about a story of yours on the bus this morning. Very exciting. I wanted to tell him I knew the author, but after I heard what he was saying I decided I'd better not." Of the three-hundred-some letters that Jackson received that summer only thirteen, mostly from friends, spoke kindly of her. "Dad and I did not care at all for your story in the *New Yorker*," her mother wrote sternly.

The reaction to the story was so severe that a front-page story in the *San Francisco Chronicle* begged to know what the story meant, and newspaper columns in New York and Chicago pointed out that *New Yorker* subscriptions "were being cancelled right and left." The *New Yorker*, then edited by Harold Ross, actually issued a press release saying that the story had resulted in more mail than any other piece of fiction ever published by the magazine. As Jackson recalled later, the letters she received represented "a kind of wide-eyed, shocked innocence." "People," she wrote, "wanted to know . . . where these lotteries were held, and whether they could go there and watch."[20]

It seems strange that a piece of fiction depicting violence could generate such a firestorm of controversy, particularly as it was published shortly after World War II; yet, it did. Just what exactly prompted so many people to write angry letters to the writer and the story's publisher? Why would a short story published in a literary magazine after one of the bloodiest conflicts in history so disturb readers?

Shirley Jackson would write later that it was very difficult to explain just what exactly she had hoped her story would say. "I supposed, I hoped, by setting a particularly brutal ancient rite in the present and in my own village," Jackson explained, "to shock the story's readers with a graphic dramatization of the pointless violence and general inhumanity in their own lives." I myself think Jackson's story was so disliked when it appeared because it is about needless suffering and the arbitrary and hands-on infliction of violence by otherwise law-abiding citizens. The idea that someone would be stoned to death, let alone by friends and neighbors as a result of drawing slips of paper out of a black box, simply offended people's collective sensibilities.[21]

The parallels between Jackson's short story and America's death penalty are, of course, inescapable: in a country of over 285 million people, America has between 15,000 and 25,000 homicides each year, yet fewer than three hundred people are sentenced to die each year. Totally innocent people are sometimes wrongfully convicted and sentenced to death, and of the 6,700 people sentenced to die in the United States from 1973 to 1999, 598—or less than 9 percent—were actually executed.[22]

All of the guilty inmates put to death committed heinous crimes, but their crimes rarely distinguish them from murderers never slated for execution. And while many Americans are now questioning the morality of any system that lets even one innocent person be sentenced to die—people in Tessie Hutchinson's position—others appear undisturbed or indifferent. Like the three-legged stool and black wooden box in Jackson's story, America's death penalty has its own customary rituals—inmates' last meals and dying declarations—and is often seen by Americans as an appropriate punishment for no better reason than because it was used by past generations. Executions—never seen by the public and conducted in a manner resembling a state-run lottery—are blindly accepted by people like Old Man Warner because, over time, they have become institutionalized in American culture.[23]

I would like to think Americans everywhere still cringe when they read stories of human brutality like the one that appeared in 2002 in the *New York Times Magazine*. An article there tells the true story of Sufiyatu Huseini, a Nigerian woman sentenced to death by stoning for adultery. "I was shattered when the judge said that," the illiterate Huseini said of her sentence, which was imposed because of her pregnant state. "I never thought there would be such a punishment," she said, breastfeeding her ten-month-old daughter, Adama. "As a Muslim," she told a reporter, "I know the laws of God are being implemented. But the law must be fair." In June 2001, an Islamic court in Sokoto, in spite of Huseini's claim that she had been raped, ordered that her sentence be carried out as soon as Adama was weaned.[24]

Under strict Islamic law, or *shari'a,* torturous punishments are commonplace in places like Nigeria. People are lashed in public for petty theft or drinking alcohol, a man's right hand is amputated for stealing a goat, a girl is publicly whipped a hundred times for having premarital sex. In one case, a man is ordered to have an eye removed for assaulting and blinding another man. Aliyu Abubakar Sanyinna, Sokoto's attorney general, coolly described the size of the stones to be thrown at Huseini. "Not big ones, moderate-sized ones—like this," he said, making a fist. Even the dean of Sokoto's law school expressed a willingness to take part. "If the state calls on someone to do his duty and carry out a law that has been properly passed, he must do it," Mansur Ibrahim Sa'id said, sitting beneath a copy of the United Nations Declaration of Human Rights taped to his office wall. "Those stoning her will be happy," he added, "because they are carrying out God's will."[25]

Fortunately, an international outcry brought Huseini's plight to light and she was never executed. When Minnesota congresswoman Betty McCollum read the article about Huseini's fate, she got the drafting assistance of an attorney at Minnesota Advocates for Human Rights and introduced a resolution in Congress condemning the sentence. "This is an extraordinarily cruel and unusual form of punishment, a gross violation of human rights," McCollum said. Under intense international pressure, an Islamic court in Nigeria overturned Huseini's death sentence on procedural grounds even as it came to light that another woman had been sentenced to death for adultery.[26]

If the plot of Shirley Jackson's fictional story is so disturbing, shouldn't the killing of real people, in a stoning pit in Nigeria or in a Texas execution chamber, shock all of us a lot more? After all, is there really any difference between death by stoning and death by lethal injection? Doesn't the use of sterilized needles simply mask the violence?

In the case of death row inmates, the use of violence against them usually just means a continuation of the cycle of violence that led to their violent acts in the first place. Johnny Garrett, executed in Texas in 1992 for killing a nun when he was seventeen, was sexually abused, was scarred from being put on a hot stove for crying, and fell off a roof when he was ten, which caused a head injury. Joseph Cannon, executed in Texas in 1998 for a crime he committed as a teenager, had head injuries from being run over by a truck at age four, suffered beatings and sexual abuse, sipped gasoline to get high, and once tried to kill himself by drinking insecticide. Clifton Belyeu himself had multiple head injuries, said he was possessed by demons, grew up in a family with a history of mental illness and abuse, and once attempted suicide.[27]

The tragic life stories of those on death row do not excuse their crimes. However, they demonstrate how easily violence in one generation can lead to violence in the next. Did it make any sense, or do any good, to end the lives of Johnny Garrett, Joseph Cannon, or Clifton Belyeu with another act of violence? I don't think so. Violence, in whatever form, has irreversible consequences and should never be used lightly or needlessly. The September 11th terrorist attacks and the string of sniper shootings in the Washington, D.C., area are just the latest examples of how violence profoundly affects us all.

If everyone treated one another with respect, there would be no need to build prisons or ever use violence. The problem, of course, is that today's world is far from an idyllic place. We live in a world inhabited by heavily armed terrorists, cold-blooded killers, and an assortment of other violent offenders, and prisons are essential to protect people from crimes of violence and to punish those who break the law. If authorities had no power to enforce a social compact—the rule of law—or bring criminals to justice, forcibly if necessary, perpetrators of violence could freely roam the streets, looting and killing people, and the result would be anarchy, the very antithesis of any organized and cultured society.

The question that any government must ask, however, is this: when is the use of violence absolutely necessary? The answer to that inquiry, I believe, is dependent on what threat of violence exists and whether the person or group posing the threat is still at large or has already been disarmed and captured.

In the case of terrorists, who already possess sophisticated weaponry and are actively planning more deadly attacks, the use of force will, at times, be necessary. Where our freedom and security are threatened, or when demented thugs seek refuge or safe haven in foreign lands after directing or carrying out criminal acts, America's military or United Nations peacekeepers have just cause to root out criminal elements. When murderers are already in custody, though, there is no justifiable need for violence to be used against them; instead, life-without-parole sentences can be imposed. There is a fundamental difference between taking responsible steps to bring armed-and-dangerous criminals to justice and taking the lives of unarmed prisoners.

To curtail violence, Americans must pay more attention to world affairs even as concrete steps are taken to reduce the availability of guns, the instruments used in so many wars and homicides. We know that children who live in homes where guns are present are at a much greater risk of homicide and suicide, and there is a clear relationship between high gun ownership rates and state homicide rates. When compared with children living in such states as Hawaii, Massachusetts, and Rhode Island, where gun ownership rates are low, children living in states where guns are more prevalent (Alabama, Louisiana, and Mississippi, for example) are three times as likely to die in a gun-related homicide. Technology and trade have made the world community more interconnected than ever before, and Americans, like everyone else, have obligations and moral responsibilities that go along with being a part of that community.[28]

In addressing the United Nations in November 2001, President George W. Bush admirably spoke of "a responsibility to deny weapons to terrorists and to actively prevent private citizens from providing them." Unfortunately, America's lax regulation of firearms—a policy promoted by Bush—does little to ensure that they do not fall into the wrong hands.

Not only can felons acquire guns with little difficulty, as evidenced by the sheer number of murders and robberies committed with firearms, but guns are found in 35 percent of all U.S. homes with children. Nearly half of those households keep firearms in an unlocked space without trigger locks, and 9 percent of those households actually keep loaded guns in unsecured places. As a result, approximately 1.7 million children have relatively easy access to deadly weapons, right in their own homes. When these statistics are considered, it certainly helps explain how emotionally damaged kids end up not in fistfights, but actually shooting people.[29]

In today's America, gun shows and concealed-carry laws make it possible for nearly anyone to obtain a gun and, in some places, freely carry it on the streets of a major city. Just four months into his first term as Texas governor, George W. Bush himself signed a bill allowing Texans to carry concealed handguns. The new law, he pledged, would make the state "a safer place," even though FBI statistics show that just the opposite is true. While Bush promised that license applicants would undergo rigorous background checks, more than four hundred people with prior convictions obtained licenses in just the first few years of the law's operation. Licensees had mental illnesses, substance abuse problems, or violent histories, including rape and armed-robbery convictions, and between January 1996 and April 2000, Texas permit holders were arrested for weapon-related offenses at a rate 66 percent higher than that of the state's general population. Of 215,000 Texans who obtained gun permits under the law from 1996 to 2000, over 3,000 were later arrested, including twenty-seven for murder, forty-nine for sexual assault, and eight for kidnapping.[30]

America's laissez-faire gun laws not only have made the commission of violent offenses more likely but also have, at times, even aided international terrorists. Among the rubble at a terrorist training facility in Afghanistan was found a manual entitled "How Can I Train Myself for Jihad" which singled out the United States for its easy availability of firearms. The Bureau of Alcohol, Tobacco, and Firearms estimates there are between 2,000 and 5,000 gun shows annually in the United States, and terrorists are known to have bought weapons at them to funnel to the Irish Republican Army, Lebanon's Hezbollah movement, and other Islamic extremist groups. In Texas alone, 472 gun shows took place in 1998. As the United States fights terrorism abroad, it's time for America to get its own house in order by enacting more stringent gun laws. This will not only make guns less available to terrorists in remote places like Afghanistan but also make it more difficult for American kids and violent felons to get their hands on deadly weapons.[31]

While the events of September 11th angered us all and steeled the world's resolve to fight international terrorism, that tragic day cannot be allowed to change our aspirations for a nonviolent society and a lasting global peace or cloud our own judgment and morality. Murderers, terrorists, and other violent offenders must be tracked down and brought to justice. However, on the home front and abroad Americans must work as never before to reduce violence and human suffering everywhere. This means both tougher state and federal regulation of guns, and fighting poverty in impoverished countries that serve as recruiting and training grounds for terrorist groups. It also means abolishing America's death penalty, an institutionalized form of violence that accomplishes nothing and merely demeans us all.[32]

Abolishing the death penalty, along with regulating guns and fighting child abuse and poverty, must be seen by Americans as being part of Martin Luther King, Jr.'s much-admired and heralded nonviolence movement. "I don't believe in the death and killing on any side," King once said, "no matter who's heading it up— whether it be America or any other country." "I've decided that I'm going to do battle for my philosophy," he declared in Mississippi in 1966. "I can't make myself believe that God wants me to hate. I'm tired of violence . . . and I'm not going to let my oppressor dictate to me what method I must use." In accepting the 1964 Nobel Peace Prize, King said everything that needs to be said: "Civilization and violence are antithetical concepts."[33]

FOUR

A Love-Hate Relationship

The overwhelming majority of Americans never use violence or hurt others in their day-to-day lives. Instead, they work hard at their jobs, regularly help those in need, and are law-abiding. Gun violence and imprisonment rates in the United States top those of other Western democracies—with one American behind bars for every 150 U.S. citizens—but Americans' ordinary activities, eating out at restaurants, traveling, or going to movies, have nothing to do with weapons or prisons. We enjoy parks and concerts, birthday and anniversary parties, sporting events, art museums and plays, reading novels and biographies, and spending time with our families. Millions of Americans volunteer their time, at churches, at homeless shelters, or by raising money for charitable causes, and we recoil in horror when we visit places like the Holocaust Memorial Museum in Washington, D.C., and see the atrocities of the past. Every year, on a national holiday, we honor the memory of Martin Luther King, Jr., and his life's work.[1]

Although we pay homage to Dr. King and the achievements of his nonviolence movement, Americans maintain a love-hate relationship with violence. We deplore violent acts when they happen in our own communities, yet all of us, I suspect, watch violent movies and TV shows from time to time. Watching action films or TV dramas like *Law and Order* and *The Sopranos* is a part of America's culture that constitutes a form of entertainment or escape that we enjoy. A lot of American kids play with harmless waterguns or watch animated cartoons full of depictions of violence, even as other parents' children are given real guns or ultraviolent video games as presents at Christmas.

When it comes to punishing convicted killers, a majority of Americans are locked in a tight embrace with a uniquely lethal form of violence: the death penalty. We abhor murder, yet, for many Americans, it is perfectly acceptable to kill murderers. In this respect, death penalty laws are singular in their approach. For example, while antidiscrimination laws make it unlawful to retaliate against those who report sexual harassment, death penalty laws allow grim retaliation, masquerading as retributive justice, against criminals. Death-row inmates' violent acts are rightfully despised, yet a large segment of Americans relish or love the thought of convicted killers being executed, whether by electrocution or lethal injection.

How did this happen? Just what exactly are the origins of death as punishment, and how did we get to where we are today? Why is it that while we strive for a nonviolent and peaceful world, we still use the ultimate form of violence, the death penalty?

Aging manuscripts, barely legible court records, and a plethora of dusty books and microfilmed newspapers trace capital punishment back as far as recorded human history goes. For millennia, societies have executed killers and others seen as deviant, sometimes for conduct that is no longer even considered a crime. The death penalty's long history is marked by prejudice, religious persecution, and at times, superstition. Bible passages and excerpts from other holy texts have long been used to justify executions, often of nonbelievers, and for a long time, public officials conducted executions only on Fridays.[2]

In the Old Testament, acts of adultery, bestiality, blasphemy, homosexuality, and murder are capital offenses, and ancient Egyptian and other legal codes sanctioned executions for a wide variety of conduct. The Babylonian Code of Hammurabi, circa 1750 B.C., made twenty-five offenses, including corruption, theft, and the fraudulent sale of beer, punishable by death. And under Roman law, killing one's father was punished by the perpetrator's being sewn up in a leather sack with a live dog, a cock, a viper, and an ape; the sack was then cast into the sea. Not long ago, executions took place in European countries such as England, France, and Germany that no longer allow the imposition of death sentences. Sixteenth-century English law recognized as capital crimes arson, burglary, larceny, murder, rape, robbery, treason, and marrying a Jew, and by the 1700s, 222 crimes, such as stealing turnips, damaging a fishpond, and associating with gypsies, were punishable by death. Common methods of execution were crucifixion, drowning, burning alive, hanging, beheading, impalement, and drawing and quartering.[3]

In the American colonies, the first execution took place in 1608 when a Virginia man, George Kendall, was killed by firing squad after being convicted of spying for the Spanish. In 1630, John Billington, a pilgrim who sailed on the *Mayflower*, became the first American hanged for murder, and in 1632 in Virginia, Jane Champion became the first woman to be executed. America's death penalty has long been authorized by statute. In 1636, the Massachusetts Bay Colony penned laws based on the Old Testament, making crimes such as idolatry, murder, perjury in a capital case, rape, rebellion, sodomy, and witchcraft punishable by death. These laws applied to adults and teenagers alike. Thomas Graunger, the first known juvenile to be executed, was put to death for bestiality in the Plymouth Colony in 1642. Before the American Revolution, public executions were not only commonplace but also often extremely gruesome spectacles. At the execution of five mutineers in New Orleans in 1754, the convicted men were strapped naked to a wheel and their bones were broken with a sledge hammer before they were left to starve.[4]

Thus, when the U.S. Constitution was ratified in 1788 and the Bill of Rights was adopted in 1791, executions were a widely accepted form of punishment. While the Italian jurist Cesare Beccaria and Dr. Benjamin Rush, a signer of the Declaration of Independence, vocally opposed capital punishment in the 1700s, the Constitution's Fifth Amendment specifically contemplates that a public body regulate the death penalty's infliction for certain crimes. "No person shall be held to answer for a *capital,* or otherwise infamous crime," it reads, "unless on a presentment or indictment of a Grand Jury." In two other places, the Fifth Amendment also puts procedural limitations on when the death penalty can be imposed: "nor shall any person be subject for the same offence to be twice put in *jeopardy of life* or limb," the amendment says, "nor be *deprived of life,* liberty, or property, *without due process of law.*" The only substantive limitation on permissible punishments is contained in the Eighth Amendment, which reads: "Excessive bail shall not be required, nor excessive fines imposed, *nor cruel and unusual punishments inflicted.*"[5]

The language of the Eighth Amendment was taken from the 1689 English Declaration of Rights, its European counterpart. Although similar words were found in Virginia's Constitution of 1776 and in eight other states, scant legislative history exists pertaining to the adoption of the Eighth Amendment as part of the Bill of Rights. All that appears in the debates of the First Congress are the objection of a South Carolina representative, "Mr. Smith," who called the words "too indefinite," and the concerns of a "Mr. Livermore" from New Hampshire. "The clause seems to express a great deal of humanity, on which account I have no objection to it; but as it seems to have no meaning in it, I do not think it nec-

essary," Livermore said. He implored that "it is sometimes necessary to hang a man, villains often deserve whipping, and perhaps
having their ears cut off; but are we in the future to be prevented
from inflicting these punishments because they are cruel?" "If a
more lenient mode of correcting vice and deterring others from
the commission of it could be invented," Livermore concluded,
"it would be very prudent in the Legislature to adopt it; but until
we have some security that this will be done, we ought not to be
restrained from making necessary laws by any declaration of this
kind." The annals of Congress merely record that, after the airing
of these two objections, the Eighth Amendment was "agreed to
by a considerable majority."[6]

Given the lack of clarity over what the Framers intended to do
by including the Eighth Amendment in the Bill of Rights, it is not
surprising that those seeking to abolish capital punishment have
fought to do so both before legislative bodies and in the courts.
The most significant battles in the U.S. Supreme Court over the
death penalty and the meaning of the Eighth Amendment were
played out in the 1970s, but efforts on legislative fronts to abolish
capital punishment began long before that. Although U.S. death
penalty opponents have had a few victories in individual statehouses and in the courts, neither approach has, thus far, resulted in
the death penalty's abolition on a nationwide basis. Thus, America's
death penalty debate continues, evolving over time even as many
of the central issues being debated remain much the same.

One of the most significant changes America's death penalty
has witnessed over the last two centuries is the demise of public
executions. In the 1800s in states such as Illinois, New York, and
Pennsylvania, abolitionists saw making executions as private as
possible a first step toward abolition and therefore pushed for laws
outlawing public executions. State legislatures began banning
these public spectacles in the 1830s and, by the 1930s, the transi-
tion was complete, with America's last public execution—that of
a black man, Rainey Bethea—taking place in 1936 in Owensboro,

Kentucky, before a crowd of up to twenty thousand people. While every state passed a law prohibiting public executions at some point between the 1830s and the 1930s, a majority of states chose to retain capital punishment. The first state law abolishing capital punishment, in fact, was not passed until 1847 in the State of Michigan and, even then, Michigan lawmakers retained death as a punishment for treason. While an 1852 law in Rhode Island banned capital punishment except for life-term prisoners convicted of murdering a guard, not until 1853 did an American state, Wisconsin, pass a law completely abolishing executions. National anti–death penalty crusaders like Marvin Bovee, the Wisconsin farmer who led that state's abolitionist drive, saw the end of public executions as a precursor to abolition, but the abolitionist movement never caught on, at least on a national scale.[7]

Legislative efforts to abolish capital punishment in the United States were often derailed by the onset of war. The 1830s to the 1850s, coinciding with the push to abolish public executions, was one of the most active abolitionist periods in American history. Antigallows societies were formed across America, and a number of legislative bodies vigorously debated the issue. But the Civil War put a stop to the grassroots movement to abolish capital punishment. No state did away with the death penalty during that war and President Abraham Lincoln, as commander-in-chief, signed many orders approving death sentences for Union army deserters. Marvin Bovee even put the publication of his anti–death penalty book, *Christ and the Gallows,* on hold during the Civil War. After the Civil War, as the historian David Brion Davis puts it, "men's finer sensibilities, which had once been revolted by the execution of a fellow human being, seemed hardened and blunted." Only three states—Iowa, Maine, and Colorado—outlawed capital punishment between 1865 and the beginning of the new century.[8]

Eventually, the abolitionist movement picked up steam, then faltered again. Between 1907 and 1917—in the Progressive Era— nine states abolished capital punishment, while American executions, as a whole, climbed to unprecedented levels. These geographically diverse states—Minnesota, North Dakota, and South Dakota in the Midwest; Kansas and Missouri in the central United States; Arizona, Oregon, and Washington in the West; and Tennessee in the South—all did away with the death penalty during peacetime. America's entry into World War I on April 6, 1917, though, spelled the death knell for the anti–death penalty movement. Although Minnesota and North Dakota never restored the death penalty after doing away with it, the tensions associated with World War I caused many state legislatures to bring back capital punishment shortly following abolition. Arizona brought back the death penalty in 1918; Missouri, Tennessee, and Washington reinstated it in 1919; and Oregon followed suit in 1920. Concerns about crime and economic hard times also triggered new death penalty laws. Kansas and South Dakota would restore the death penalty in 1935 and 1939, respectively, in close proximity to the Great Depression and the beginning of World War II.[9]

The willingness of Americans to use the death penalty has, in spite of statute books authorizing its infliction, fluctuated greatly over time. In the 1930s, the number of persons executed each year by civil authorities in the United States ranged anywhere from 140 in 1932 to 199 in 1935. The 1940s saw a slight decrease, with annual executions ranging from a low of 117 in 1945 to a high of 153 in 1947. Not until the 1950s did executions begin to slow down, with the number of annual executions dipping below one hundred for each year of that decade, except for 1951, which saw 105 executions. The next two decades saw executions decline even more dramatically. In the tumultuous 1960s and early 1970s, the number of executions fell to all-time lows. In 1960, there were fifty-six executions; in 1962, forty-seven; in 1964, fifteen; seven in 1965; one in 1966; and two in 1967. There would be no executions at all in the United States from 1968 through 1976.[10]

The precipitous decline in executions and the de facto moratorium on them that began in 1968 set the stage for the U.S.

Supreme Court's landmark decision in *Furman v. Georgia*. That case involved three black defendants, one convicted of murder and two convicted of rape; the victims were all white. In its 1972 *Furman* decision, the nation's highest court held that the death penalty's imposition on William Furman, Lucious Jackson, and Elmer Branch constituted "cruel and unusual punishment" in violation of the Constitution. The judgment of the Supreme Court was delivered in a terse, six-sentence per curiam opinion followed by the words "So ordered." So divided was the Court, however, on the rationale for its judgment, that, in more than 230 pages of concurring and dissenting opinions, each of the nine justices wrote and filed a separate opinion.[11]

The justices' views were as diverse as the views of the American people with respect to the death penalty itself. Justice William Douglas, appointed to the Court by Franklin Roosevelt, wrote that "one searches our chronicles in vain for the execution of any member of the affluent strata of this society." "People live or die, depending on the whim of one man or of twelve," Douglas wrote, fearful the death penalty was being "selectively applied" by judges and juries based on "prejudices" against "poor" and "minority" defendants. Douglas concluded that a law discriminatory in application "has no more sanctity than a law" that, for instance, said "that blacks, those who never went beyond the fifth grade in school, those who made less than $3,000 a year . . . should be the only people executed." Justice Douglas declared death penalty laws "unconstitutional in their operation" because he found them "not compatible with the idea of equal protection of the laws that is implicit in the ban on 'cruel and unusual' punishments."[12]

Justice William Brennan, citing earlier Court rulings, emphasized that the Eighth Amendment "must draw its meaning from the evolving standards of decency that mark the progress of a maturing society." In such prior cases, the Court had ruled that "punishments of torture" like beheading, breaking on the wheel, burning alive, crucifixion, and public dissection would run afoul of the Eighth Amendment and that it was "cruel and unusual punishment" to deprive a wartime U.S. Army deserter of his citizenship or put a prisoner in chains for twelve years at hard labor. In 1890, the Court had held that electrocutions were constitutional, but Brennan concluded in his opinion in *Furman* that "uncivilized and inhuman punishments" that do not "comport with human dignity" violate the Eighth Amendment. Even though the Court had previously ruled that punishments involving "the mere extinguishment of life" were not unconstitutional, Brennan wrote that the "calculated killing of a human being" is "uniquely degrading to human dignity." In distinguishing 1970s America from the 1770s, Brennan argued that at the time of the country's founding, "without developed prison systems, there was frequently no workable alternative" to death sentences.[13]

As part of the Court's 5–4 majority, Justice Brennan wrote that, while the Framers certainly saw death as a common punishment, "the further inference that they intended to exempt this particular punishment from the express prohibition of the Cruel and Unusual Punishments Clause" could not be made. "If anything," Brennan argued, "the indication is to the contrary, for Livermore specifically mentioned death as a candidate for future proscription under the Clause." Justice Brennan also saw the death penalty as totally at odds with basic principles of fairness. "No one," he emphasized, "now contends that the reference in the Fifth Amendment to 'jeopardy of . . . limb' provides perpetual constitutional sanction for such corporal punishments as branding and earcropping, which were common punishments when the Bill of Rights was adopted." "When a country of over 200 million people inflicts an unusually severe punishment no more than 50 times a year," Brennan said, "it is being inflicted arbitrarily."[14]

Other jurists echoed Brennan's approach. "These death sentences are cruel and unusual in the same way that being struck by lightning is cruel and unusual," Justice Potter Stewart said in a concurring opinion. Considering "all the people convicted of rapes and murders," he said, he saw the three condemned men before the Court as "a capriciously selected random handful." Allowing the death penalty to be "so freakishly imposed," Stewart concluded, violates the Eighth Amendment. Justice Byron White also opined that "the death penalty is exacted with great infrequency even for the most atrocious crimes and that there is no meaningful basis for distinguishing the few cases in which it is imposed from the many cases in which it is not."[15]

Justice Thurgood Marshall, in his opinion, emphasized up front that the "criminal acts with which we are confronted are ugly, vicious, reprehensible acts." "Their sheer brutality cannot and should not be minimized," he said. Yet Marshall, writing as the only minority on the Court, was appalled "that innocent people have been executed before their innocence can be proved" and that "Negroes were executed far more often than whites in proportion to their percentage of the population." Citing Mr. Livermore's congressional remarks, Marshall emphasized that the "cruel and unusual punishments" prohibition is a "flexible" concept "that may change in meaning as the mores of a society change, and that may eventually bar certain punishments not barred when the Constitution was adopted." Marshall found capital punishment "excessive" and "morally unacceptable to the people of the United States at this time in their history"; thus, he too found death penalty laws unconstitutional.[16]

Justices Warren Burger, Harry Blackmun, Lewis Powell, and William Rehnquist all dissented in *Furman*. If "possessed of legislative authority," Burger wrote, he would either vote to outlaw the death penalty or "restrict" its use "to a small category of the most heinous crimes." All four dissenting justices called the Eighth Amendment's "cruel and unusual punishments" clause "one of the most difficult to translate into judicially manageable terms," but stated that "the explicit language of the Constitution affirmatively acknowledges the legal power to impose capital punishment." The justices stated that "punishments such as branding and cutting off of ears, which were commonplace at the time of the adoption of the Constitution, passed from the penal scene without judicial intervention because they became basically offensive to the people and the legislatures responded to this sentiment." "Beyond any doubt," they wrote, "if we were today called upon to review such punishments, we would find them excessively cruel because we could say with complete assurance that contemporary society universally rejects such bizarre penalties." Emphasizing that death penalty laws remained on the books of forty States, the District of Columbia, and under federal law, the four dissenters said that there are "no obvious indications that capital punishment offends the conscience of society to such a degree that our traditional deference to the legislative judgment must be abandoned."[17]

The four dissenters in *Furman* were particularly troubled by what they saw as the Court's abrupt reversal in course. Just a year earlier, in *McGautha v. California,* the Court had held that, under the Fourteenth Amendment's due process clause, death sentences could be handed out by jurors as they saw fit. "In light of history, experience, and the present limitations on human knowledge," the Court in *McGautha* held, "we find it quite impossible to say that committing to the untrammeled discretion of the jury the power to pronounce life or death in capital cases is offensive to anything in the Constitution." "*McGautha* was an exceedingly difficult case," the *Furman* dissenters argued, saying "reasonable men could fairly disagree as to the result." "If stare decisis means anything," they wrote, referring to the legal principle counseling adherence to precedent, *McGautha* "should be regarded as a controlling pronouncement of law." "This pattern of decision-making," they said, "will do little to inspire confidence in the stability of the law." Conceding that "human error" was unavoidable, Justice Rehnquist nevertheless lamented that the *Furman* ruling struck down "a penalty that our Nation's legislators have thought necessary since our country was founded."[18]

In a separate dissent, Justice Harry Blackmun wrote that death penalty cases were, for him, "an excruciating agony of the spirit." "I yield to no one in the depth of my distaste, antipathy, and, indeed, abhorrence, for the death penalty," he said, adding that while he personally rejoiced at the Court's ruling, he felt that the Court "overstepped." "Capital punishment serves no useful purpose that can be demonstrated," Blackmun wrote. "For me," he said, "it violates childhood's training and life's experiences, and is not compatible with the philosophical convictions I have been able to develop." The death penalty, he noted, "had never been a part of life" for him because in his home state, Minnesota, "it just did not exist." "Were I a legislator," Blackmun explained, "I would do all I could to sponsor and to vote for legislation abolishing the death penalty." But Blackmun felt constrained by his role as judge. "We should not allow our personal preferences as to the wisdom of legislative and congressional action, or our distaste for such action, to guide our judicial decision in cases such as these," he wrote.[19]

The *Furman* decision—a narrow, if clear, abolitionist victory—did much more than save three men from execution. Because the nation's other death row inmates had been convicted under equally defective death penalty laws, the *Furman* decision invalidated their death sentences too. In all, over six hundred inmates had their death sentences set aside, and many people predicted that America had seen its last execution.[20]

However, the death penalty's abolition never came to pass. Thirty-five states quickly passed new death penalty laws, and just four years later, the U.S. Supreme Court felt compelled to address the issue again. In *Gregg v. Georgia* and two companion cases handed down on July 2, 1976, the eve of America's bicentennial celebration, the Court upheld death sentences from Georgia, Texas, and Florida. "Despite the continuing debate, dating back to the 19th century, over the morality and utility of capital punishment," the Court wrote, "it is now evident that a large proportion of American society continues to regard it as an appropriate and necessary criminal sanction." While the Court struck down mandatory death penalty laws in Louisiana and North Carolina, ruling that sentences less than death at least had to be considered, the new statutory schemes in Florida, Georgia, and Texas were ruled constitutional. The laws in those states, the Court said, sufficiently guided jurors' discretion over life-and-death decisions so as to comply with *Furman*'s mandate that death sentences not be inflicted arbitrarily.[21]

Since *Gregg*, the U.S. Supreme Court has decided a number of cases that narrowed the kinds of offenders who are death eligible. In *Coker v. Georgia*, it held that a death sentence for rape violates the Eighth Amendment's guarantee against "cruel and unusual punishments" where the victim is not killed. In *Enmund v. Florida*, it reversed a death sentence where the evidence disclosed only that the defendant was the driver of a getaway car. In *Ford v. Wainwright*, it held that the Eighth Amendment prohibits the execution of the insane. And in *Thompson v. Oklahoma*, the Court refused to approve the execution of a fifteen-year-old offender.[22]

Yet, in the years following *Furman*, other, more broad-based challenges to America's death penalty were rejected by the nation's highest court. In the consolidated cases of *Stanford v. Kentucky* and *Wilkins v. Missouri*, the Court refused to set aside the death sentences of sixteen- and seventeen-year-old offenders. In *Penry v. Lynaugh*, the Court refused to say that the Eighth Amendment prohibits the execution of the mentally retarded. And in *McCleskey v. Kemp*, it ruled that statistical evidence showing that Georgia's death penalty is administered in a racially discriminatory fashion did not render a black man's death sentence unconstitutional. "Apparent disparities in sentencing are an inevitable part of our criminal justice system," the Court held in its controversial 5–4 decision. Only in 2002, after eighteen states had outlawed the execution of the mentally retarded, did the Court, in *Atkins v. Virginia*, overrule *Penry* and hand down another decision, *Ring v. Arizona*, that called a large number of death sentences into question. In *Ring*, the Court set aside Arizona's death penalty law and ruled that, under the Constitution, jurors, not judges, must make the requisite factual findings before defendants are sentenced to die.[23]

The *Atkins* and *Ring* rulings showed the U.S. Supreme Court's willingness to reconsider its approach to death penalty cases. However, that doesn't change the fact that many of the Court's prior decisions erected almost insurmountable procedural barriers—what my former teacher, Joseph Hoffmann, calls "excessive proceduralism"—designed to prevent the substantive review of death penalty cases altogether. In *Coleman v. Thompson*, the Court ruled in 1991 that where a Virginia death row inmate's notice of appeal was filed three days late by his lawyer, his claims were procedurally defaulted and could not be raised at all in federal court. Although Justice Blackmun dissented, calling the Court's rules "a Byzantine morass of arbitrary, unnecessary, and unjustifiable impediments to the vindication of federal rights," the majority opinion said the case was about "federalism" and "finality" even though a man's life was at stake. In another case, *Murray v. Giarratano*, the Court held that death row inmates have no constitutional right to lawyers in habeas corpus proceedings even though condemned inmates must often wait until then to claim a trial lawyer was incompetent. And in *Teague v. Lane*, the Court ruled that "new rules" of constitutional law will generally not be applied retroactively to cases on collateral review, thus barring their universal application.[24]

These rulings make it extremely onerous for prisoners to get death sentences reviewed, let alone reversed, and the complex rules often mean courts spend more time deciding if they can even hear a case than they actually spend looking at the merits of a claim. The "procedural default" doctrine precludes federal courts from reviewing claims when a defendant's lawyer has failed to comply with state procedural rules, and the Supreme Court has made it easier for courts to apply the "harmless error" rule to constitutional violations. In a 1992 case, the Court even tightened the standard for obtaining evidentiary hearings, making it more difficult for prisoners to have their claims heard at all.

The maze of procedural barriers in habeas corpus cases has shifted the focus of judges away from assessing whether an inmate's constitutional rights have been violated to whether procedural rules preclude relief.[25]

These kinds of rulings lead to what the American writer Joseph Heller dubbed Catch-22s, where sought-after outcomes are impossible to attain because of illogical rules. A defendant, untrained in the law and perhaps illiterate, does not know how to raise claims and objections he must assert in order to preserve them because he has an incompetent lawyer; if and when the defendant, now on death row, finally receives assistance from a new lawyer, the claims or objections cannot be raised either because they are barred by a statute of limitations or because they are deemed waived; if the new lawyer makes costly mistakes in a habeas corpus proceeding, the client can raise no challenge to those potentially fatal errors either, because the U.S. Supreme Court says death row inmates are not entitled to lawyers in habeas corpus proceedings in the first place.[26]

This system often produces bizarre results. Judge Donald Lay, a federal appellate court jurist who has spoken to my students, is just one of many people who are extremely troubled by the law's focus on procedural issues. "It is difficult for many of us to believe," Lay says, as a member of a court that hears death penalty cases, "that in today's society an individual may be executed by reason of technical error by his or her lawyer in order to exalt the goal of state finality above the requirements of fundamental fairness." "It is indeed a sick society," Lay concludes, "that executes its youth, ill, mentally retarded, and paraplegic prisoners without considering their constitutional claims, simply because their lawyers failed to file timely appeals or made other procedural errors."[27]

As it is, the U.S. Supreme Court can review only a small number of claims. The Court receives over eight thousand certiorari petitions a year, of which it agrees to hear roughly eighty cases.

Of those, just a handful—perhaps three or four a year—are capital appeals. Individual members of the U.S. Supreme Court often have expressed reservations about the death penalty's morality over the years. In 2001, for example, Justice Ruth Bader Ginsburg said she supports a death penalty moratorium because of the poor quality of lawyers she sees in capital cases. The Court as a body, however, has shown a willingness on many occasions simply to wash its hands of state-sanctioned killing by, in effect, deferring to state court judgments.[28]

A major turning point in the U.S. Supreme Court's approach to death penalty cases came in 1992 when members of the Court stayed up all night just to ensure that California's first execution in twenty-five years went ahead. In that case, California's governor, Pete Wilson, had already denied Robert Alton Harris's clemency petition even though he acknowledged that Harris, who murdered two teenagers, had suffered "monstrous child abuse." In what Governor Wilson called a "macabre legal circus" performed by "manipulative lawyers and indulgent judges," Harris was brought into the gas chamber, then taken out of it, before he was gassed. His lawyers had obtained a final stay of execution from a Ninth Circuit judge at 3:51 A.M. after a long night of legal wrangling that saw four separate stays issued by the lower federal courts, but failed to get the Supreme Court to take a closer look at the case. At 8:45 A.M. Eastern time, a frustrated Supreme Court actually enjoined the lower federal courts from further interfering with the execution, originally scheduled for one minute after midnight. Although lower court judges wanted more time to consider Harris's claims, the Supreme Court simply wanted the execution to go forward.[29]

The Supreme Court's unwillingness to outlaw death sentences means that the battle over capital punishment will have to be fought in state legislatures, in Congress, and in the court of public opinion. I am optimistic that one day America's death penalty will be relegated to the past. However, if that is to happen, death penalty opponents must continue to speak out and reframe the debate.

Murderers are, of course, unpopular and always will be. Consequently, if the death penalty debate continues to be seen as a contest of wills between convicted killers and murder victims and their families, unseen executions will never stop. The public, rightfully outraged by murders and violent crime, will always favor victims' rights over saving the lives of convicted killers.

To succeed, death penalty foes must convince politicians and voters to stop seeing the death penalty as a crime-fighting tool, which it clearly is not, as Texas's high murder rate illustrates perfectly. Death penalty opponents must make the electorate see executions for what they really are: just another form of violence in our society. If capital punishment is seen as being totally at odds with the principles of nonviolence, and if people start to think about how executions affect *our own values*—as opposed to what they do *to convicted killers*—they may be more receptive to doing away with them.

I am realistic enough to know that death penalty opponents face an uphill battle in the years to come. There are many good, well-intentioned people who believe that the death penalty should be retained, and death penalty opponents must convince those voters that they should have a change of heart, just as the Reverend Carroll Pickett has. A chaplain to Texas death row inmates for fifteen years, Pickett ministered to ninety-five men in their last hours on death row. "Like so many Texans," he says, "I was raised in an atmosphere that insisted the only real justice was that which claimed an eye for an eye." "I was wrong," he admits now, saying that as he participated in the execution process, "I found myself wondering just what we were accomplishing." The fact that public executions are no longer in use makes winning converts even more difficult because such spectacles used to naturally draw people into the abolitionist movement.[30]

In hindsight, it is clear now that nineteenth-century death

penalty foes made a calculated, if understandable, error. They supported laws banning public executions, reasoning that if executions were not publicized, death penalty advocates would be forced to concede that capital punishment served no deterrent function—which was, at the time, one of the primary justifications for the death penalty's use. With no publicity for executions, they reasoned, capital punishment soon would be abolished. After all, if executions were not conducted publicly, how could they possibly deter crime, and, if they did not deter crime, why would anyone want them?[31]

But this approach backfired, and America's death penalty remains a fact of life. Instead of leading to the death penalty's abolition, these laws—the predecessors of laws banning television cameras from executions—led to apathy among the general public. Because today's executions are not seen, the death penalty issue has been largely relegated to the back burner of American politics.

The film *Dead Man Walking* and the tireless efforts of civic and religious leaders such as Sister Helen Prejean have, in large measure, reawakened America's anti–death penalty movement. One poll done in 2000, a joint effort by Republican and Democratic polling firms, showed that overall support for the death penalty had slipped to 60 percent, with 64 percent of respondents supportive of a moratorium on capital punishment. Indeed, although the tragic events of September 11th may have temporarily stalled the momentum of America's abolitionist movement, it has not taken Americans too long to begin asking the same troubling questions they were asking before that fateful day.[32]

In the year 2002 alone, Maryland's governor Parris Glendening put a moratorium on executions in that state; in a New York case, U.S. District Judge Jed Rakoff struck down the federal death penalty as unconstitutional because so many death row inmates were later found to be innocent; and U.S. Senators Russ Feingold and Jon Corzine pushed for a moratorium on federal executions. "With each new death penalty statute enacted and each execution carried out," Senator Feingold once said when speaking in favor of another bill, the Federal Death Penalty Abolition Act, "our executive, judicial, and legislative branches, at both the State and Federal level, add to a culture of violence and killing." "With each person executed," he said on the Senate floor, "we are teaching our children that the way to settle scores is through violence, even to the point of taking a human life." Judge Rakoff, in finding the Federal Death Penalty Act unconstitutional because DNA tests showed an "undue risk" of executing innocent people, was even more blunt. "The unacceptably high rate at which innocent persons are convicted of capital crimes, when coupled with the frequently prolonged delays before such errors are detected," he ruled, "compels the conclusion that execution under the Federal Death Penalty Act, by cutting off the opportunity for exoneration, denies due process and, indeed, is tantamount to foreseeable, state-sponsored murder of innocent human beings."[33]

Calling executions "legalized hatred," Sister Prejean tells audiences around the country about the executions she has witnessed and the murderers and murder victims' families she has counseled. I find her message compelling. "Beyond the rhetoric of all the legislators who score their political points for being tough on crime," she says, "what it all boils down to is that a handful of people are hired to kill a guy in the middle of the night." "We imitate the very violence that we say we can't have," she tells church groups and whoever will come to listen to her speak. Murder victims and their families must never be forgotten by the criminal justice system, and those affected by violent crimes must always, I believe, be allowed to speak their minds and express their anger and pain at sentencing hearings. Indeed, the impact of a crime cannot be assessed properly without hearing from those most affected by it, and victims and their families certainly deserve to have their voices heard in criminal cases. At the same time, however, under no circumstances should the judicial system itself be made into a tool of violence, to be used to kill people in our own names.[34]

No doubt, the most significant event in the political arena for abolitionists before September 11th came when, in 2000, Illinois Governor George Ryan, a conservative Republican, declared a moratorium on executions in his home state. After thirteen Illinois death row inmates were exonerated by new evidence, Ryan said he would not allow any more executions unless an appointed panel could give him "a one hundred percent guarantee" against any mistaken convictions. "Until I can be sure with moral certainty that no innocent man or woman is facing a lethal injection," Ryan announced, "no one will meet that fate." Ryan described the system as "so fraught with error" that it almost caused "the ultimate nightmare, the State's taking of innocent life." "I'm not sure the system can be fixed," the once-staunch death penalty supporter told an audience.[35]

The September 11th terrorist attacks have, in some ways, complicated things for the abolitionist movement. In their views on the death penalty, many capital punishment supporters make distinctions between terrorists and mass murderers, on the one hand, and, on the other, killers who murder a single victim. Executing terrorists and serial killers should be allowed, some say, even as they reject death sentences for other murderers. The challenge facing those who deplore capital punishment is to convince enough people, including our nation's leaders, that the use of violence against incarcerated killers is wrongheaded because life-without-parole sentences can more than adequately protect the public.

As law enforcement agencies and America's soldiers grapple with how best to root out and bring heavily armed terrorists to justice, Americans themselves face a choice. Are they going to continue their illicit love affair with the death penalty, or will they chart a new, less violent course for America's legal system? In short, will we continue to execute murderers and terrorists— who use violence—or reject the violence of executions and impose life-without-parole sentences in their place?

As part of America's quest for a nonviolent society, we must, of course, do everything we can to prevent and guard against future terrorist attacks. So long as terrorists remain on the loose, the United States government and law enforcement personnel in foreign countries and across America will have work to do. However, our efforts to stop violence must not end there. Instead of putting needles into imprisoned criminals who do not share our value for human life, Americans should focus their energies on real solutions to reducing violence, like tougher gun laws. Killing the perpetrators of violence does nothing but make for more violence, while better regulation of firearms may actually save lives. The abolition of America's death penalty is just one way already within our grasp to reduce violence, and we should do just that and do away with this barbaric form of punishment.

FIVE

The Machinery of Death

America's death penalty often resembles a well-oiled machine. In a process governed by written rules of procedure, indictments are handed down, motions and court papers are filed with clerks' offices, and execution dates are set. At the postconviction stage of a case, today's laws often set extremely short deadlines for the filing of habeas corpus petitions. Virginia, an active death penalty state, has what is called the "twenty-one-day rule," which gives anyone convicted of a crime a mere three weeks after sentencing to bring forward any newly discovered evidence. The doctrines of procedural default and statute of limitations are mechanically applied to bar death row inmates' claims, and prisoners are executed as a result of court orders deposited in the U.S. mail or sent over fax machines to lawyers and wardens.[1]

People, not machines, however, run each stage of the death penalty process. It is individual police officers who investigate crime scenes and individual forensics experts who evaluate evidence. It is individual prosecutors who charge cases, individual public defenders or private attorneys who defend clients, individual witnesses who give in-court testimony, and twelve-person juries who determine guilt or innocence. And it is judges and governors with names and life stories who sign papers that seal prisoners' fates, and individual correctional officers who pull the switch at executions. No human being is ever infallible, and, thus, each stage of a death penalty case—from investigation to execution, both of which can be botched—offers opportunities for mistakes to occur.

Many actors in the criminal justice system freely admit—as does Gerald Kogan, a former chief justice of the Florida Supreme Court and an ex-prosecutor who used to ask juries to return death verdicts—that the death penalty system is so fraught with error that it should be abolished. "This is the ultimate penalty," Kogan says, "and too many mistakes are being made." Others, however, are in denial or prefer to gloss over the frequent media reports of incompetent attorneys, bungled investigations, or intentional misconduct, like the Oklahoma police chemist who fabricated testimony in a series of criminal cases. George W. Bush, for instance, expresses confidence that no innocent inmates were ever executed during his gubernatorial tenure. "I know there are some in the country who don't care for the death penalty," he once said on the campaign trail, "but I've said once and I've said a lot, that in every case, we've adequately answered innocence or guilt."[2]

One of more than one hundred executions that Bush let go forward as Texas governor was that of Gary Graham, who was convicted of killing a man in a May 13, 1981, holdup at around 9:30 P.M. outside a Houston supermarket. Graham was seventeen at the time of the offense. The perpetrator left the scene of the crime without being apprehended, and two eyewitnesses were unable to identify the killer because they did not get a good enough look at him. Graham pled guilty to ten aggravated robberies that took place from May 14 through May 20, 1981, but his capital murder conviction was based solely on the testimony of a single eyewitness. Defense counsel presented no evidence at the guilt/innocence phase of Graham's trial, and the testimony of three alibi witnesses was rejected as not credible in a subsequent habeas corpus proceeding. The U.S. Supreme Court voted 5–4 to let the execution proceed in 2000 even though other witnesses had come forward to support Graham's innocence claim, and a Houston police report indicated that the .22 caliber pistol Graham had with him when he was arrested was not the .22 caliber pistol used in the killing. "I analyze each case that comes across my desk and look at the innocence and guilt of each person," Bush told reporters when he refused to intervene. "After considering all of the facts I am convinced justice is being done," he said. "May God bless the victim, the family of the victim, and may God bless Mr. Graham."[3]

For a man who didn't trust county-level vote counters to hand-tally Florida presidential ballots, Bush's remarks about Graham's guilt, even if true, put, I think, far too much faith in the ability of Texas's judicial system—or any death penalty system, for that matter—to assess guilt or innocence accurately. A new Texas law, put in place by Bush in 1995, makes that system even more unreliable. That law requires convicted persons to apply for habeas relief no later than forty-five days after filing briefs on direct appeals, meaning that state habeas petitions must be filed while direct appeals are still pending. Applications filed after that forty-five-day period are considered untimely and rejected. To make matters worse, Texas trial judges often conduct only "paper hearings" in state habeas proceedings where no live testimony—let alone cross-examination of witnesses—is permitted. The Texas Court of Criminal Appeals frequently rubber-stamps lower court rulings, which are often verbatim copies of prosecutors' proposed findings, in unpublished, one-page orders.[4]

While executions are, more and more, being expedited by state legislatures and the courts, the secretive, star-chamber nature of executions continues to perpetuate countless myths about capital punishment. In order to lay bare the innermost workings of America's death penalty machine, these myths must be dispelled.[5]

Myth #1: Innocent people aren't executed.

False. A study published in the *Stanford Law Review* in 1987 found that since 1900 at least twenty-three people who were likely or potentially innocent have been put to death. And the wrongful convictions just keep piling up.[6]

Walter McMillian, a black man accused of murdering a white woman in Alabama, was locked up on death row even before his conviction and was sentenced to death at a one-and-a-half-day trial. The jury rejected the testimony of a half-dozen black witnesses who said McMillian was at a fish fry at the time of the murder. Instead, jurors accepted the testimony of a murderer who testified falsely against McMillian, a man known in his rural community to have had an interracial extramarital affair. Only because McMillian had a stellar postconviction lawyer, who proved evidence was withheld from the defense, was McMillian exonerated in 1993 after spending nearly six years on death row. McMillian's lawyer actually unearthed a tape recording on which the prosecutor's chief witness told police McMillian had nothing to do with the crime.[7]

Over one hundred people, in fact, have been released from death row since 1973 because of serious doubts about their guilt or because DNA or other evidence conclusively proved their innocence. For example, Kirk Bloodsworth and Ronald Williamson were freed from Maryland and Oklahoma death rows after each spent nine years in prison for murder-rapes they did not commit. Bloodsworth, a former marine with no arrest record, was convicted of raping a nine-year-old girl on the basis of mistaken eyewitness identifications, and the lawyer who represented Williamson had never tried a capital case. Earl Washington, a black man with an IQ of 69, spent a decade on Virginia's death row for a rape and murder he never carried out. Although Washington had confessed to the murder, he was pardoned in 2000 after DNA testing cleared him. While housed at Virginia's Mecklenburg Correctional Center, Washington had once come within days of being executed.[8]

In Illinois, Republican Governor George Ryan's moratorium on executions was imposed when the number of death row inmates exonerated in that state climbed to thirteen, exceeding the twelve executions that, since 1977, had taken place there. Rolando Cruz endured three murder trials and spent over twelve years in prison for the kidnapping, rape, and murder of ten-year-old Jeanine Nicarico before a police officer came forward and admitted lying under oath. The Ford Heights Four, two of whom were sentenced to death in Illinois for the 1978 murder of a suburban couple, collectively spent over sixty-two years in prison before their release; in 1999, the four black men, who sued for violation of their civil rights, received a $36 million settlement for their wrongful imprisonment.[9]

Anthony Porter, a black man who spent sixteen years on Illinois's death row, was also mistakenly convicted and sentenced to die. Once just forty-eight hours away from execution, Porter obtained a stay of his execution only because a psychologist's test showed an IQ of 50, raising serious questions about his competency. Only later did Northwestern University journalism students locate evidence proving Porter's innocence, which led to the conviction of another man who confessed to the crime.[10]

A few death row inmates have come within hours—or minutes—of execution only to be released from prison when new evidence came to light. In Florida, Joseph Green Brown was released from death row in 1987 after spending thirteen years there. He had once come within fifteen hours of execution before a court found that a prosecutor had knowingly allowed a witness to lie. In 1915 and 1942, Charles Stielow and William Wellman were both strapped into electric chairs when gubernatorial reprieves arrived in the nick of time. Stielow was pardoned and released from prison after the real culprit confessed, and Wellman, a black man from North Carolina, was freed after another man admitted committing the crime, the rape of a white woman. Authorities discovered that, on the day of the rape, Wellman was 350 miles away from the scene of the offense. On some occasions, governors have actually posthumously pardoned executed persons, and on others, the supposed homicide "victim" was found alive after an execution took place.[11]

The reasons miscarriages of justice occur in the criminal justice system are as varied as they are disturbing. Confessions used at trials are later found to have been coerced by police or made by mentally ill defendants. Pressure to solve homicides and prosecutorial misconduct also result in errors, and the cause of death is sometimes erroneously assessed. Suicides and accidents, for example, are mistakenly classified as murders, leading to convictions in cases where charges should never have been filed in the first place. In other instances, key prosecution witnesses lie to avoid prosecution or the death penalty themselves, or they have faulty memories. The largest category of all errors in wrongful convictions is, in fact, misidentifications.

It is often people outside the criminal justice system—journalists or ordinary citizens—who uncover the truth. The filmmaker Errol Morris stumbled upon the Texas case of Randall Adams only by chance. His documentary *The Thin Blue Line* generated national interest in Adams's case and led to Adams's 1989 release after he had been sentenced to death and spent more than a decade in prison. Randall Adams, who had come within one week of being executed, was represented at trial by a real estate lawyer.[12]

Myth #2: Death row inmates all get fair trials.

Not so. Condemned inmates have been represented by intoxicated attorneys and lawyers who fell asleep in court or called their own clients "wetbacks" or "niggers." The *Chicago Tribune* found that thirty-three people sentenced to die in Illinois were represented by attorneys who were later disbarred or suspended from the practice of law. Lawyers less than a year out of law school have been appointed to defend capital cases, and incompetent attorneys have failed to hire investigators or experts, present evidence of a defendant's schizophrenia, or put on any evidence at all at the penalty phase of a capital case. In one Texas case, all the attorney said at sentencing was "You are an extremely intelligent jury. You've got that man's life in your hands. You can take it or not. That's all I have to say." That attorney was later suspended, but the consequences for his client were far more severe: execution. Another Texas lawyer, who has seen at least a dozen of his clients end up on death row, boasted in an interview that he had flunked criminal law and drank a lot of whiskey with judges. "I have a permanent parking spot at the grievance committee," that lawyer said of his many bar-related reprimands.[13]

Court-appointed attorneys, often handpicked by state court judges who have no desire to conduct long trials with lots of experts, are often paid less than twenty dollars per hour, and attorneys in rural parts of Texas have been paid less than nine hundred dollars to defend a capital case. A study in Virginia found that the effective hourly rate paid to those who represented indigent defendants in capital cases was thirteen dollars per hour. Some states even impose caps on lawyer compensation. The limit is twenty-five hundred dollars in Kentucky, and Alabama sets the maximum payment at two thousand dollars; a challenge to Mississippi's limit of one thousand dollars per case was rebuffed by that state's supreme court.[14]

At Clifton Belyeu's trial, two woefully unprepared lawyers represented him. A federal judge later found that the lawyers rendered constitutionally "deficient" performance at the sentencing phase of Belyeu's trial by "failing to investigate or present evidence in mitigation of psychiatric or neurological disorders." Yet U.S. District Judge Walter Smith—and the U.S. Court of Appeals for the Fifth Circuit—let Belyeu's execution go forward anyway on the ground that Belyeu somehow suffered no "prejudice" by virtue of the lawyers' abysmal performance.[15]

Other stories are just as troubling. After John Sullivan ended up on Louisiana's death row, attorneys at Dorsey & Whitney, Minnesota's largest law firm, agreed to take on the case. They discovered that Sullivan's trial lawyer spent just ten and a half hours preparing for trial and failed even to make an opening statement, and that the entire trial was completed in just one day. "We spend more time preparing to try a misdemeanor case," Minneapolis attorney Tamara Byram would say later, after the U.S. Supreme Court agreed to hear Sullivan's case and granted a new trial. Though Sullivan was convicted in 1982 of a murder in New Orleans, he sat on death row for eight years before an appeal was even filed on his behalf. "He was literally not doing anything until the court ordered him to do it," Byram said of Sullivan's appellate lawyer.[16]

The whole process by which defendants in Texas and elsewhere are sentenced to death is, from beginning to end, appalling. During jury selection in one capital case, a judge in Texas started fixing two Colt revolvers on the bench with a screwdriver. When attorney Sandra Babcock drafted a 250-page brief detailing new evidence in another case, the judge denied relief the very next day. "I'm convinced he didn't read it," Babcock says. The state's former governor, George W. Bush, decided that thirty minutes was too long to spend on a final review of a death sentence, so he cut final reviews to a mere fifteen minutes. A former French justice minister, Robert Badinter, was so disturbed by Bush's oversight of (and lack of oversight of) more than a hundred Texas executions that he called Bush "the world champion executioner."[17]

As Stephen Bright, the director of the Southern Center for Human Rights, recently wrote, "A person may be condemned to die in Texas in a process that has the integrity of a professional wrestling match." In a country where nearly three hundred death sentences are imposed each year, the prevailing attitude in places like Texas, Bright laments, reflects "a Western macho thing, the justice of the Marlboro man." In 1997, the American Bar Association itself called for a moratorium on all executions, calling the death penalty system "a haphazard maze of unfair practices."[18]

Myth #3: The death penalty is reserved for the most heinous crimes.

It's not. Thousands of murders are committed in America

every year, yet fewer than one hundred people are put to death each year. While the serial killers Ted Bundy and John Wayne Gacy and terrorist Timothy McVeigh were executed, other convicted terrorists and multiple murderers are never sentenced to die. More often than not, it is those who kill someone in the course of a robbery or a burglary who get sentenced to death and, even then, only a random handful of such criminals get executed.[19]

The vast majority of capital offenders, it turns out, are really no different from other convicted killers facing life or lesser sentences. A study of 558 inmates whose death sentences were set aside by the Supreme Court's *Furman v. Georgia* decision found that *Furman*-commuted inmates who remained incarcerated committed six killings—four of prisoners and two of guards—in the institutional setting. Of the 239 paroled offenders, post-release records showed that one killed again and that two rapists raped again. These recidivism rates are comparable to those of other convicted murderers—only a tiny percentage of whom commit a subsequent homicide—and the study found that four of the *Furman*-commuted inmates were innocent and that almost 99 percent, or 551, of the inmates did not kill again.[20]

Decision-making prosecutors in death penalty states, over 97 percent of whom are white, have unbridled discretion to seek (or choose not to seek) death sentences. This results in stark geographic and racial disparities in sentencing outcomes. While death penalty states averaged 3.9 death sentences per 100,000 people from 1973 to 1995, a few localities are responsible for a disproportionate number of death sentences. Over two-thirds of American counties have not imposed the death penalty since 1976, while just 3 percent of the nation's 3,066 counties account for half of the country's death sentences. In the southern Virginia town of Danville, population 50,000, nine of twenty-three capital crimes from 1978 to 1997 resulted in death sentences. In other Virginia jurisdictions, death sentences were handed out in just 5 percent of capital cases. Almost one-third of American executions take place in Texas, and roughly one-third of Texas's death row inmates originate out of one locale, Harris County, where a local prosecutor, Johnny B. Holmes, made capital charging into a cottage industry. Just five of ninety-four federal jurisdictions account for 40 percent of death penalty prosecutions by federal prosecutors.[21]

While a few prosecutors, such as Bronx District Attorney Robert Johnson, refuse to seek death sentences, others, such as Harry Connick, Sr., of New Orleans, routinely do. The prosecutor in Philadelphia, Lynne Abraham, files capital charges virtually as often as the law permits. As a result, Philadelphia County has the third-largest death row population in the country, exceeded only by Texas's Harris County and California's Los Angeles County. After the execution of Keith Zettlemoyer, the first man executed in a northeastern state since 1967, Lynne Abraham told a reporter, "It was a nonevent for me. I don't feel anything." "When it comes to the death penalty," she says, "I truly believe it is manifestly correct." When asked about a man who spent four years on death row after being framed, Abraham could reply only, "He wasn't executed. The system worked."[22]

Some prosecutors seek death sentences out of fear that, if they do not, dangerous criminals might be released back into society someday. The longtime prosecutor in Danville, Virginia, William Fuller believes that "the legislature is supposed to legislate, the courts are supposed to interpret, and I'm supposed to apply the law faithfully." "These cases really tear at me," he says of the capital cases he prosecutes. "I'm not some cold-blooded person who isn't bothered by this." "In most of these capital cases I tried," he says, "parole eligibility was fifteen years, and we had liberal parole boards, so you just had to seek the death penalty." Only since life-without-parole became a viable option in Virginia has Fuller felt less pressure to seek death sentences.[23]

Myth #4: There's no discrimination in the death penalty's administration.

Not true. Between 1930 and 1990, 53 percent of the 4,016 people executed in the United States were black, and from 1930 to 1976, when blacks made up just 12 percent of the U.S. population, 90 percent of all rapists executed were black. In the South, where Jim Crow laws once mandated racial segregation, whites and blacks—going back to the days of slavery—routinely received different punishments for similar crimes. From 1600 to 1949, 588 African Americans were executed in the South for rape, compared with 48 white rapists. Over 80 percent of modern-day executions take place in the South, where slavery was legalized until the Confederacy lost the Civil War, and racial discrimination in capital cases has been documented by the federal government's General Accounting Office and by scholars around the country. In federal death penalty cases, 75 percent of defendants are minorities.[24]

In places where executions are prevalent today, extrajudicial lynchings used to be quite common as well. Lynchings, of course, were often racially motivated. Of the 4,743 lynchings that took place in America between 1882 and 1968, over 72 percent were of blacks. While minorities now receive criminal trials, the substitution of state-sanctioned executions for lynchings has not done away with the racist views still held by some. Though lynch mobs are no longer part of America's landscape, the result of executions and lynchings—death—is the same. "The death penalty," writes lawyer Stephen Bright, who has spent many years in Southern courtrooms, is really nothing more than "a direct descendant of lynching and other forms of racial violence and racial oppression in America."[25]

In fact, today's death sentences are over four times more likely to be imposed on murderers whose victims were white than on those whose victims were black. A new study on racial disparities in death penalty cases in Philadelphia—the City of Brotherly Love—found that black defendants are nearly four times more likely than other defendants to be sentenced to death, even when the circumstances of the slayings are similar. Especially in southern "Death Belt" states such as Florida, Texas, and Virginia, where most executions take place, racist attitudes still remain as vestiges of the days of illegal lynchings and Ku Klux Klan rallies. When murder victims are white instead of nonwhite, death sentences are 5.5 times more likely in Mississippi, 4.8 times more likely in Florida, 4.3 times more likely in Georgia and Oklahoma, and 3.5 times more likely in North Carolina.[26]

Myth #5: The death penalty is cheaper than life-without-parole sentences.

Not true either. In Texas, a typical death penalty case costs $2.3 million, three times the cost of imprisoning someone in a single cell at a maximum-security prison for forty years. In Florida, death sentences cost over $3 million, compared with $516,000 for a life sentence, and in North Carolina, they cost at least $2 million more per execution than life-without-parole sentences. Indiana's Criminal Law Study Commission found that it costs at least 30 percent more to execute a criminal than it does to impose a life-without-parole sentence, and a recent study done in California showed that taxpayers would save $90 million a year by abolishing the death penalty. People forget that it costs more money to pay judges and lawyers bent on killing people than it does to pay for prison guards.[27]

Myth #6: Impartial jurors hand out death sentences.

False. In a process sanctioned by the U.S. Supreme Court, all capital juries are "death qualified," meaning death penalty opponents are excluded from sitting in judgment in capital trials. This makes capital juries more conviction-prone and also stacks the deck against criminal defendants at the penalty phase of capital trials, where verdicts must often be unanimous. A judge in Texas told a writer for the *New Yorker* that it takes about three weeks to pick a jury in a capital case. "It takes that long to cull out the people who can't give the death penalty," the judge said.[28]

Another result of death-qualifying capital juries is that a disproportionate number of women and minorities are excluded from them. "A trial is 90 percent jury selection," says Michael

McGovern, a former homicide prosecutor. "My perception is that minorities tend to say much more often that they are opposed to the death penalty. Prosecutors are aware of that. A lot of Latinos and blacks will be lost on these questions." Public opinion polls confirm McGovern's observation. While roughly 70 percent of whites support capital punishment, fewer than 50 percent of non-whites tell pollsters they do. Women also are considerably less likely to voice support for the death penalty. The exclusion of a disproportionate number of women and minorities from juries has undoubtedly affected the outcome in at least some criminal cases. A study of capital juries in South Carolina, for example, found that white jurors are roughly twice as likely to cast their first ballot vote for death as are black jurors. Ironically, while death penalty opponents are regularly excluded from juries, the U.S. Supreme Court uses jury verdicts to gauge society's "evolving standards of decency"—the very standard used to assess the death penalty's constitutionality in the first place.[29]

Many jurors, if given better information and the opportunity to impose life-without-parole sentences, might not even want to hand out death sentences. An eleven-state study of capital juries showed that four of five jurors agreed with the statement that "persons sentenced to prison for murder in this state are back on the streets far too soon." Those jurors, however, routinely underestimated exactly how long a defendant would be incarcerated if not sentenced to death. In all eleven states, citizens' release estimates for murderers fell below—often far below—the mandatory minimum sentences required by state law. Defendants are thus sentenced to die by jurors on the basis of misinformation. Studies have consistently shown that the sooner jurors think a defendant will get out of prison, the more likely they are to vote for death.[30]

To make matters worse, state laws frequently ask jurors to weigh "aggravating" versus "mitigating" factors to decide between life and death in what resembles a mechanical, almost mathematical calculation. In a process designed to help jurors distance themselves from the moral decisions they are being asked to make, prospective jurors are asked repeatedly if they can "follow the law." Even before guilt is established, they are asked during jury selection if they will be able to impose death sentences, suggesting that this is what the law expects of them.[31]

A review of 280 Georgia trial transcripts found that seventy death sentences were returned only after jurors asked specific questions of the court regarding the nature of life imprisonment. "Is there life without parole?" one jury asked pointedly. Unfortunately, because state laws frequently forbade judges from telling juries if a defendant would be eligible for parole under a "life" sentence, defendants were often condemned to die on the basis of faulty information about sentencing alternatives. At the 1985 trial of James Randall Rogers, jurors specifically asked if he would be eligible for parole if given a life sentence. Thirty-four minutes after the judge refused to answer the question, jurors returned a death sentence. "We really felt like we didn't have any alternative," one juror said later. Not until 1994 did the U.S. Supreme Court rule that jurors in a capital case must be told if a defendant would never be eligible for release where the defendant's future dangerousness is at issue.[32]

Only a few jurors actually feel any personal responsibility for death sentences. In one study, over 81 percent of surveyed jurors in capital cases placed "foremost responsibility" for these sentences on the defendant or "the law." In some cases, prosecutors freely encourage jurors to abdicate their sense of responsibility for their decisions. During jury selection in Peter Miniel's case, one juror, Patrick O'Rourke, said that the death penalty needed to be "speeded up," even if it meant the execution of innocent people, and the decision to execute someone was "more or less a mechanical process." Even so, the prosecutor told O'Rourke during voir dire that Miniel would either be executed or retried "ten years from today" and only after "fifty judges"—from the Texas Court of Criminal Appeals, the United States Supreme Court, and various state and federal courts—reviewed his case. Miniel, convicted in 1988, still sits on Texas's death row.[33]

Myth #7: Death sentences are a better deterrent than life without parole.

Again, not true. Statistics from active death penalty states show how ludicrous it is to say that the death penalty deters or reduces violent crime more effectively than incarceration. In two active death penalty states, Louisiana and Texas, firearm-related injuries have sometimes exceeded injuries from motor vehicle crashes, and from 1979 to 1987, those states ranked third and fifth, respectively, in gun deaths. In 1997, Louisiana had 15.7 murders per 100,000 people; by comparison, Minnesota's murder rate was 2.6 per 100,000 residents. Texas has one of the country's worst records when it comes to violent crime. From 1988 to 2000, 1,608,276 violent crimes, including 23,795 murders, were reported in Texas; in that thirteen-year period, there were 674.5 violent crimes per year and, on average, over 10 murders a year per 100,000 state residents. A study of the 1,588 homicides in Minnesota from 1985 to 1997 showed that handguns—as is the case in other states—were the most prevalent homicide weapon; however, over that thirteen-year period, Minnesota's homicide rate was far lower than that of Texas, ranging from two to four homicides annually per 100,000 people.[34]

The U.S. homicide rate has regularly surpassed that of western European countries, at times by a 4-to-1 margin. For example, in 1997, the homicide rate in England and Wales, where gun ownership rates are low, was 1.3 murders per 100,000 people. While Canada's murder rate was slightly higher that year, at 1.7 homicides per 100,000 people, the United States had 6.8 homicides per 100,000 people. In 1990, when the U.S. murder rate was 9.4 per 100,000 people, the rates in western Europe were much lower: 1.5 per 100,000 in Sweden and Great Britain, 1.1 per 100,000 in France, and 0.9 per 100,000 in the Netherlands. From 1997 to 1999, the European Union averaged 1.7 homicides per 100,000 residents, a rate far lower than America's murder rate over that same time frame. The lesson is clear: the death penalty does not help reduce violent crime.[35]

In the United States, high murder rates must be seen as a major public health issue. Homicide is the leading cause of death among African American males aged fifteen to twenty-four and is the third leading cause of death among young males regardless of race or ethnicity. Only motor vehicle accidents and cancer claim more kids' lives. While homicide rates fell by 41 percent from 1991 to 1999, research shows that violent crime rates are driven not by death penalty laws but by such factors as the availability of semi-automatic handguns among those under age twenty-five, the level of education of a given population, and household income. Men with fewer than nine years of education die from homicide at 9.5 times the rate of male college graduates. Men with family incomes below five thousand dollars are almost nine times as likely to be murdered as men with incomes of twenty-five thousand dollars or more, and inner-city residents are at much greater risk of being murdered than those living outside central cities. Persons living in the South, where executions are most frequent, are, by far, more at risk for homicide than persons living in other regions of the country. Economic conditions and turf wars over crack cocaine markets may explain homicide rates, but when a state executes people, it clearly does not help to reduce violent crime rates.[36]

Theoretically, executions can both deter and provoke violent crime, as deterrent and brutalizing effects are not mutually exclusive. Recent social science research confirms, though, that the death penalty's overall effect is only to brutalize a society by teaching its members that the use of violence is acceptable. Studies of executions and homicide rates in Arizona, California, Illinois, New York, Pennsylvania, and South Carolina all show increases in homicides after state-sanctioned executions, making the net effect of executions more, not fewer, murders.[37]

The very idea that, in a death penalty state, a typical killer would, before murdering someone, rationally weigh the consequences of his or her actions, or conduct a cost-benefit analysis as to the chances of being executed, rings hollow. Most homicides, facilitated by easy access to guns, are acts of passion carried out during heated arguments or intrafamilial conflicts or while the offender is drunk or on drugs. Over half of all homicides are carried out by people while under the influence of alcohol, and a survey of state prison inmates found that more than 40 percent of violent offenders, as a group, were using alcohol or alcohol with drugs when they committed their offenses. The average amount of ethanol they consumed before their offenses was more than nine ounces—the equivalent of three six-packs of beer. Of the violent offenders, 46 percent had abused drugs in the month preceding the offense, and 29 percent had engaged in a pattern of daily drinking in the year before it. Those who kill or pull out a knife or gun and put other lives at risk by trying to provoke the use of deadly force—an action known as "suicide by cop"—are far more likely to be despondent over a lost job or relationship, acting in blind rage, or be seeking money for drugs, than they are to be thinking about what a state or federal law may say as regards capital punishment.[38]

A study of London homicides and twenty-two notorious executions in England between 1858 and 1921 found that "executions encourage homicides" and that "the publicity accorded an execution adds to its brutalizing effect." The data showed that, for the twenty-two executions studied, there were 271 homicides in the ten weeks before the executions, as compared to 324 homicides in the ten weeks after the executions. The study reached the disturbing conclusion that "the brutalizing effect" of executions is "stronger in impact than any deterrent effect that may occur."[39]

These findings should come as no surprise, because they merely provide scientific proof for what civic leaders recognized over one hundred years ago: executions do not prevent violence; if anything, they incite it. The reason that American executions were moved into prisons beginning in the 1830s was that pick-pocketing, drunkenness, and violent crime occurred at, or right after, public executions. Legislators knew that these public spectacles were not making communities any safer, and they banned them to stop the lawlessness and unruly behavior spawned by hangings at high noon in the public square. Many states passed nighttime execution laws at the same time to further reduce public access to information about executions, fearing that the information itself might provoke crime.[40]

Because polling data show that over 40 percent of Americans continue to believe that the death penalty deters crime, the deterrence myth needs to be dispelled so that those who cling to it will come to see the death penalty as counterproductive. The views of experts—most criminologists and police chiefs agree that the death penalty does not reduce homicides and is just a symbolic way for politicians to show how "tough on crime" they are—are persuasive all by themselves. However, an examination of American history also confirms that the death penalty is not helpful in reducing violent crime.[41]

The very notion that executions might deter crime was rejected outright by American legislators more than a century ago. Indeed, the widespread nineteenth-century belief that well-publicized executions were injurious to society explains why, starting in the 1880s, state legislatures actually passed "gag" or "muzzle" laws that forbade the very publication of execution details in newspapers. Such laws, enacted in Arkansas, Colorado, Minnesota, New York, Virginia, and Washington, made it unlawful to print anything other than the mere fact that an execution had taken place. Newspapers could print the date and time of a convict's death, but nothing more. Violators of these gag laws could be criminally prosecuted—as they were in Minnesota and New York—for simply reporting news. If public executions were harmful to the public, legislators believed that news stories about executions were too, if only less so.[42]

In 1907, the Minnesota Supreme Court went so far as to uphold

the constitutionality of one of these gag laws, dubbed the "midnight assassination law" because it required private, after-dark
executions. The court explicitly ruled that the intent of the law
was "to surround the execution of criminals with as much secrecy as possible, in order to avoid exciting an unwholesome effect on the public mind." The court held that to advance the law's
purpose of "avoiding publicity," executions "must take place before dawn, while the masses are at rest, and within an enclosure,
so as to debar the morbidly curious." Lawmakers and the courts
recognized that executions were demoralizing and wanted the
public to hear nothing of them.[43]

Other nations' political leaders also have resoundingly rejected
the deterrence argument and done away with capital punishment,
often despite popular sentiment for it at the time. For example, in
Canada, Great Britain, and Germany, roughly two-thirds of the
public actually opposed abolition when it took place in those
countries. American politicians, by contrast, have retained capital
punishment laws, often citing its "deterrent" value even though
scientific studies show no support for such assertions. While
other nations have moved into the twenty-first century without
death as a punishment for crime, what Americans have been left
with as a result of a lack of political leadership is an archaic death
penalty machine, broken beyond repair.[44]

In spite of the chilling congressional testimony of wrongfully
convicted men like Walter McMillian, wrenched from his family
and friends and—in his words—put in a cell "the size of a shoe-
box with no sunlight," America's death penalty machinery grinds
on. In fact, the U.S. Supreme Court has, over the past twenty-five
years, often shown indifference or callousness to the plight of
death row inmates, rejecting claims of innocence and deprivation
of constitutional rights despite serious or lingering questions
raised by the evidence. In a 2002 case, *Bell v. Cone*, the Court upheld the death sentence of Tennessee inmate Gary Cone, even
though his lawyer suffered from a mental illness, later committed

suicide, and presented no mitigating evidence or final argument on Cone's behalf at the penalty phase of the trial. During its 2002 term, the Court also refused to set aside the death sentence of a Virginia man, Walter Mickens, who was represented at trial by a lawyer who had represented the murder victim in that case on assault and concealed-weapons charges at the time of the murder. In June 2002, Mickens was executed after Virginia's governor denied his request for clemency. A large number of habeas corpus petitions have been thrown out by the Court not on the merits, but because the Court has erected procedural roadblocks to preclude the review of death row inmates' claims.[45]

Despite all the effort to grease the wheels of justice, the error rate in death penalty cases is nothing short of astounding. A recent study led by James Liebman, a professor at Columbia Law School, shows just how many mistakes are made in death cases. That study looked at 4,578 capital sentences reviewed by state appellate courts and 599 capital sentences reviewed in federal habeas proceedings from 1973 to 1995. It found that 5,760 death sentences were imposed in the United States during that time, yet executions for the study period numbered 313, or 5.4 percent of the total. Of the 4,578 death sentences reviewed on direct appeal by a state's highest court, 1,885, or 41 percent, were tossed out due to serious error. Even more death sentences were vacated in state habeas corpus proceedings, and of the 599 death sentences reviewed by the federal courts, 237, or 40 percent, were set aside because of potentially fatal errors. In those instances, it took on average more than seven years to detect the errors. Incompetent defense lawyers were responsible for 37 percent of the mistakes, 20 percent of the errors involved faulty jury instructions, and 19 percent of the errors—the third largest category—were due to police or prosecutorial misconduct. At retrials, 75 percent of the convicts whose death sentences were vacated got lesser sentences and, in a number of cases, acquittals were the outcome. The overall error rate from 1973 to 1995 in capital cases was 68 percent.[46]

Although life-endangering errors are the norm in capital cases, Congress added over fifty death-eligible offenses to federal law in 1994, discontinued funding capital defense resource centers in 1995, and drastically curtailed prisoners' habeas corpus rights. The Antiterrorism and Effective Death Penalty Act of 1996, enacted after 1995's Oklahoma City bombing, put even more obstacles in the path of prisoners trying to obtain relief in federal court. That law put in place a one-year statute of limitations for filing federal habeas corpus petitions, requires federal judges to give greater deference to state court rulings, curtails the availability of appellate review, and restricts the filing of successive petitions. The intent of the law is to speed up executions, and it accomplishes that objective by creating almost insurmountable procedural barriers to obtaining habeas relief. While over 90 percent of death row inmates are indigent and need appointed counsel, American states are still not required to pay for postconviction lawyers despite the shortage of attorneys willing to handle these cases.[47]

Though many death row inmates have no representation at all, a small cadre of attorneys work year after year, in an often hostile climate, to put a wrench in the cogs of the machinery of death. Some of these lawyers work in death penalty states such as Georgia, at Stephen Bright's Atlanta-based Southern Center for Human Rights. Others hail from places like Minnesota, far from where capital cases are actually litigated in court. These attorneys must travel hundreds of miles to investigate their clients' cases, track down as-yet-unlocated medical records, work with mental health experts, and find witnesses who may cast new light on a case or recant trial testimony. These lawyers have walked the corridors of death row, and the stories they tell only reinforce my own opposition to capital punishment.[48]

Jim Volling, the lawyer I worked with on Clifton Belyeu's case, represented convicted killer David Wilson in postconviction proceedings in the 1980s. A black man convicted of killing a white victim, Wilson had an IQ of 66. He grew up in extreme poverty, dropped out of school in the ninth grade without ever learning to read or write, and had childhood convulsions that often went untreated. After regular run-ins with the juvenile justice system, Wilson was placed in a foster home for boys, from which he ran away repeatedly, stealing to support himself. A psychiatric report done when he was seventeen diagnosed him as a paranoid schizophrenic, and after multiple convictions for burglary and robbery, his family members severed ties with him.[49]

At trial, Wilson was represented by attorney John Simmons. The prosecution's evidence showed that Wilson was traveling on Interstate 10 on October 17, 1983, with two companions, Larry Benjamin and Larry Taylor. When the car ran out of gas near Slidell, Louisiana, Benjamin urged Wilson not to "do anything drastic." The evidence showed, however, that Wilson exited the car carrying a sawed-off shotgun and hid in tall grass on the shoulder of the road. When a passing motorist, Stephen Stinson, stopped to offer assistance, Wilson emerged from the tall grass, shoved the shotgun into Stinson's face, and fired at point-blank range. Although Wilson testified he was asleep in Taylor's car during the incident, police found blood on Wilson's clothing and shotgun shells in his pocket, directly contradicting his testimony. Wilson was on parole in California for second-degree burglary and was returning from a trip to seek reconciliation with his parents in Alabama at the time of the murder. Unfortunately, at no point before trial did Simmons, Wilson's trial lawyer, look into his client's long history of mental illness.[50]

Only after Jim Volling got involved was David Wilson's death sentence reexamined. After exhaustively reviewing Wilson's medical records and assessing his mental state, clinical psychologist Marc Zimmerman concluded Wilson is mentally retarded. Another medical expert, Jonathan Pincus, found that Wilson's childhood home had many guns in it and that Wilson had burn marks on his skin and scars all over his back and chest. Pincus determined Wilson had been shot at as a child and that he was beaten "with a bull whip, 2x4's, a hose, pipes, a tree approximately 4 inches in diameter, wire, a piece of steel and belt buckles." To avoid the abuse, Wilson sometimes lived outside in the fields for as long as two weeks at a time, relying on a relative to covertly bring food to him. After reconsidering the case, a federal court ordered an evidentiary hearing to determine if Wilson's trial lawyer committed prejudicial errors by not interposing an "insanity defense" or challenging Wilson's competency to stand trial. Eventually, Wilson's death sentence was vacated.[51]

Almost invariably, it seems, those on death row have severe mental illnesses or are retarded or mentally impaired. In the 1990s, Minneapolis lawyer Bruce Peterson—now a judge—led a team of lawyers representing Florida death row inmate Donald Gunsby, who was convicted of murdering Hesham Mohammad Awadallah at a grocery store. Gunsby read at the fourth-grade level and had an IQ of less than 59. At Gunsby's 1988 trial, witnesses testified that Gunsby left a party after hearing about a friend's altercation with an Iranian proprietor of a store. According to trial testimony, Gunsby fired a shotgun, killing the proprietor's brother, then fled as three pistol shots were fired at him. One witness testified that, before leaving the party, Gunsby said he was "tired of those damn Iranians messing with the black." He was later picked out of a photo lineup and identified at trial by the convenience store's cashier clerk and the murder victim's brother.[52]

Peterson's firm took on the case after the Florida Supreme Court affirmed Gunsby's murder conviction and, on a narrow 4–3 vote, his death sentence. While alibi witnesses testified at trial that Gunsby was not at the scene of the crime when it occurred and a police officer testified that the victim's father had identified another man as the murderer, the Florida Supreme Court, on direct review, did not question Gunsby's guilt. The only contentious issue was whether Gunsby should be put to death in light of his mental state. "Gunsby's mind operates at the level of a child," a dissenting justice determined, calling Gunsby "delusional" and "a seriously emotionally disturbed man-child." Hoping to stop the execution of a mentally retarded man, Peterson's firm undertook to investigate Gunsby's life and reinvestigate the crime for which he was convicted.[53]

Peterson discovered that Gunsby was represented at trial by a court-appointed solo practitioner, Edward Scott, out of law school for less than a year. Scott had never handled a first-degree murder case, failed to object at trial to false statements about Gunsby's criminal record, and spent just thirteen hours preparing for the trial's penalty phase. Jurors "never found out" Gunsby "suffered from organic brain damage because that evidence was never presented to the jury by his attorney," Circuit Judge Thomas Sawaya ruled six years after Gunsby's trial. Gunsby "does not know how many months are in a year or in what direction the sun rises," Sawaya ruled. Gunsby, raised in former slave quarters in rural Florida, had no birth certificate or driver's license, leading Peterson to describe him as an "invisible man."[54]

A seasoned lawyer, Peterson grew to believe that Donald Gunsby might be innocent and that what had been portrayed at trial as a racially motivated murder at a mom-and-pop convenience store might, in fact, have been a drug-related murder committed by rival drug dealers. Although at trial two eyewitnesses had identified Gunsby as the murderer and others had said he made incriminating statements about the murder, Gunsby's new Minneapolis attorneys unearthed a host of new evidence. The husband of one eyewitness admitted his wife told him she did not see who shot the victim because the gunman was wearing a mask. That eyewitness was also found to be romantically involved with one of the original murder suspects. Another eyewitness, who never testified at trial at all, was located and confirmed that the shooter was wearing a pantyhose mask, as were other assailants involved in the crime. The original Florida Supreme Court opinion affirming Gunsby's death sentence did not even mention other assailants, let alone say that they were wearing masks.[55]

Also, Peterson's firm discovered that the murder victim's

brother—one of the state's key witnesses—had drug, burglary, and stolen-property charges pending against him when he fingered Gunsby as the murderer. These criminal charges were never disclosed to Gunsby's trial attorney. Florida prosecutors also failed to disclose that another key witness was arrested for violating her parole before testifying against Gunsby. "What the State did in withholding this information was wrong," a state circuit judge ruled later, calling the prosecution's "misconduct" inexcusable. In subsequent habeas corpus proceedings, the Florida Supreme Court found that Gunsby's constitutional rights were violated not only by the poor performance of Gunsby's trial lawyer but also because "the State failed to disclose the criminal records of two key witnesses." Ultimately, the Florida Supreme Court overturned Gunsby's conviction and ordered a retrial, concluding that "confidence in the outcome of Gunsby's original trial" was lacking. The new evidence "undermined the credibility of several key witnesses who testified at trial," the court ruled.[56]

On the retrial in 1997, Gunsby was convicted again, though no death sentence was imposed. Though important legal issues remained at stake, Gunsby's conviction was affirmed without comment by Florida's appellate court. In Minneapolis, Bruce Peterson continues to wonder whether an innocent man sits in prison.[57]

Another Minnesota lawyer, Steve Pincus, tells an even more disturbing story, that of Albert Burrell's kafkaesque legal odyssey. While he was a commercial litigator at the Minneapolis law firm of Lindquist & Vennum, Steve Pincus and another lawyer, Chuck Lloyd, spent hundreds of hours over nearly ten years until they proved Burrell's innocence. A Louisiana man, Albert Burrell languished on death row for thirteen years before his release from the Angola State Penitentiary in 2001. Remarkably, a denim jacket, a ten dollar check, and a tersely worded release memo from the warden were all the State of Louisiana gave Burrell when he was set free.[58]

The murder Albert Burrell was convicted of in 1987 happened

on Labor Day weekend the year before. The victims, William and Callie Frost, were an elderly couple who lived near Downsville, Louisiana, where they subsisted mainly on social security and the sale of home-grown watermelons. They were both shot in the head, and the Frosts' suitcase, which they stored under the bed, was missing; because the suitcase was thought to contain what little money they had, the suspected motive for the killings was robbery. From the outset, though, police had little to go on and botched the investigation. No fingerprints were found, and the only footprint at the crime scene was destroyed when authorities tried to make a plaster cast of it. The FBI offered to help, but the local parish's sheriff, Larry Averitt, would not accept their assistance.[59]

Six weeks after the murders, investigators got what they believed to be their first solid lead when Albert Burrell's ex-wife, Janet, called Sheriff Averitt at home. After her divorce, Janet Burrell had married Albert's brother, James Burrell, but still held a grudge against Albert, who had gotten custody of their son. Janet told the sheriff she met Albert twice on the day before the Frosts' bodies were found to talk about their son and that, at a prearranged 8:30 P.M. meeting on a rural road, Albert told her he couldn't stay but would be back at 11:00 P.M. Janet said that when Albert finally showed up at 11:30 P.M., she got in his car and found a wallet which she claimed had Mr. Frost's driver's license and social security card in it. She also claimed that Albert told her he had shot into the Frosts' house, broken down the door, and taken Mr. Frost's wallet and over two dozen hundred dollar bills. Based on these allegations and Janet's additional statement that she had seen blood on Albert's boots, Albert Burrell was arrested.[60]

After Burrell's arrest, another man, Michael Graham, was arrested as well. Kenneth St. Clair, other members of the St. Clair family, and Amy Opal, a teenage girl who was a houseguest of that family, gave statements to the effect that Graham and Burrell had been seen together at the St. Clair home on the night of the murders, that Graham had blood on his arm and shirt, and that the two men were counting money out of a suitcase. This evidence got Burrell and Graham indicted for murdering the Frosts, and, shortly following the indictment, Olan Wayne Brantley, a prisoner who shared a jail cell with Graham, told the sheriff's office that Graham had admitted that Burrell and Graham had killed the Frosts.[61]

Aided by the jailhouse snitch's testimony, the district attorney's office tried Graham's case, and he was found guilty and sentenced to death. Brantley later claimed to have had a conversation with Albert Burrell on July 26, 1987, in which Burrell supposedly confessed to the murders and asked Brantley to help him cut a deal with the district attorney on his behalf. When coupled with Janet Burrell's testimony, Brantley's testimony led to Burrell's first-degree murder conviction and a cell on Louisiana's death row. Burrell's defense lawyer at trial was later disbarred after he was convicted of narcotics offenses and his cocounsel was also disbarred for acts of dishonesty, fraud, and deceit. The law firm of Lindquist & Vennum got involved only after Burrell's new trial motions were denied, the Louisiana Supreme Court upheld his death sentence, and the U.S. Supreme Court denied Burrell's petition for a writ of certiorari. "I didn't have nothing to do with them two old people. I didn't kill anyone," Burrell repeatedly told his new lawyers once they started representing him.[62]

When subjected to scrutiny, the prosecution's case against Albert Burrell slowly unraveled. Burrell's new lawyers spoke with Dan Grady, the assistant district attorney who prosecuted Graham and Burrell, and Grady disclosed he had recommended against even prosecuting the two cases because the evidence, in his opinion, "was too weak and too dependent upon witnesses of questionable credibility." "Notwithstanding my advice," Grady stated in a 1995 affidavit, "the district attorney directed me to present the cases to the grand jury and to try them to avoid embarrassment to the sheriff." Burrell's new lawyers also learned that, while the murder investigation was under way in 1986, Sheriff Averitt engaged in acts that brought a federal indictment alleging he conspired to defraud Union Parish and a guilty plea to mail fraud.[63]

It was the impeachment of the prosecution's star witnesses, however, that ultimately led to Albert Burrell's release. Shortly after Burrell's trial, his ex-wife, Janet, recanted her testimony, saying she lied to get Albert in trouble and gain custody of their child. But when a new trial motion was heard, she refused to repeat her recantation and again adopted her trial testimony. An affidavit she signed in 1998 explained her abrupt switch in stories. "What I told the police was not true," Janet Burrell swore in the affidavit, saying, "I did not see Albert Ronnie Burrell at all on the night that the Frosts were killed." When she told sheriff's deputies she had lied, she attested, "they threatened me" and "told me if I had provided them information that was not true and changed my story, they could take my son away from me forever and put me in jail." Janet's husband, James Burrell, also recanted his trial testimony, swearing in an affidavit that "on the night that the Frosts were killed, my wife Janet was with me the entire evening."[64]

Pincus and Lloyd also discovered that Olan Wayne Brantley's nickname in the community is "Lying" Wayne Brantley. Brantley had passed a number of bad checks and in 1981 had been found not guilty by reason of insanity on the charge of issuing a worthless check. After being released from the Central Louisiana State Hospital later that year, Brantley was found incompetent to stand trial on charges brought in 1982, and in 1986, on yet another charge, witnesses noted Brantley's propensity to tell "fantastic stories." Brantley was taking medication during Albert Burrell's trial, had forgery charges reduced to the lesser charges of issuing worthless checks upon coming forward with evidence against Burrell and Graham and, after the two trials, was jailed again in Florida. Incredibly, using aliases, the mentally ill Brantley told

Florida authorities that two other capital murder defendants had confessed to him. Brantley also claimed to be friends with the jailed mob figure John Gotti, a member of the Gambino crime family, to be dating the singer Tanya Tucker, and to be a member of families that own the Grand Ole Opry, the NFL's Houston Oilers, and the NBA's San Antonio Spurs.[65]

The trial testimony of the four members of the St. Clair family, as well as Amy Opal, was also discredited. Lindquist & Vennum's investigation revealed that the prosecution failed to disclose to Burrell's and Graham's defense lawyers pretrial statements made by the St. Clairs that differed substantially from their trial testimony. In one of the statements the St. Clairs said Graham and Burrell were at their home on Saturday, August 30, and that they were sure it was Saturday night because they were watching wrestling. The murders, however, happened on August 31, a Sunday night. The pretrial statements also raised other inconsistencies on crucial pieces of evidence, such as whether Graham had blood on him and the amount of money Burrell allegedly had. Amy Opal gave an affidavit in which she totally recanted her trial testimony. She said that Jackie St. Clair told her, "Say this, say that. Don't tell about my brother." In the affidavit, she said she was afraid of the St. Clairs and that it was Kenneth St. Clair, once a suspect, whom she saw with blood on him. Ultimately, in a written submission that led to Graham's and Burrell's release, the State of Louisiana concluded that there was "a total lack of credible evidence linking Graham and/or Burrell to the crime."[66]

Oftentimes, however, a lawyer is unable to prove a client's innocence. In such cases, all the attorney can really do is try to save the prisoner's life. Minneapolis lawyer John Getsinger, for example, did just that in a Louisiana case, by getting Alvin Scott Loyd's death sentence vacated and replaced with a life sentence. The crime was particularly horrendous—the rape and murder of a three-year-old girl—but Loyd's sanity, as in so many killings, was very much at issue from the start. Only after an initial determination that Loyd was not competent to stand trial was that finding reversed and Loyd put on trial and convicted of first-degree murder in the toddler's death. Although his death sentence was set aside, Loyd no longer poses a threat to the general public. He will be spending the rest of his life behind bars in a Louisiana prison.[67]

Though many death sentences are overturned on appeal, America's death penalty system is nothing but unpredictable, and courts often refuse to stop executions from taking place. After Twin Cities' lawyer Tom Fraser began representing Louisiana death row inmate Dobie Gillis Williams, convicted of killing Sonja Knippers after hiding in her bathroom, a federal district judge ordered a new sentencing hearing. Williams's trial lawyer, the judge concluded, provided ineffective assistance of counsel at the penalty phase of Williams's trial by failing to present any mitigating evidence despite Williams's long history of mental health problems. The U.S. Court of Appeals for the Fifth Circuit, however, reversed that ruling and reinstated Williams's death sentence. That court also rejected as procedurally barred Williams's claim of discrimination based on the fact that no black foreman had been selected in the fifteen years before his indictment in the parish in which he was sentenced to die. With Sister Helen Prejean serving as his spiritual advisor, Williams was executed in 1999. Although many people believe Williams is guilty, others are not so sure. "For the first time," Sister Helen Prejean has said of Williams, "I believe I befriended a truly innocent man on death row."[68]

Sometimes, a lawyer can only take solace in a dissenting opinion or the knowledge that he or she did everything possible to save the prisoner's life. Joe Margulies, Betty Lou Beets's lawyer for eleven years, just happened to be the same lawyer who was standing by a Texas fax machine when, in 1994, Justice Harry Blackmun's remarkable dissent in *Callins v. Collins* came across it. Having witnessed the execution of his long-time client—a woman born to an alcoholic father, raped at age five, and savagely abused by a series of violent husbands—Margulies is no stranger to death row inmates' lives. He came to know how Beets's father beat her with his fists and a belt buckle, how her spouses hit, raped, or bit her, and how Beets drank heavily, during one period drinking up to five cases of beer every week. Indeed, Margulies has, for more than a decade, represented death row inmates, calling troubled men such as James Billiot and Joe Cordova his clients. Cordova, an alcoholic, committed a murder after drinking heavily on the night of the offense, and Billiot was convicted of using an eight-pound sledgehammer on Thanksgiving Day in 1981 to bludgeon to death his mother, stepfather, and stepsister. The day that Black-mun's dissenting opinion in *Callins* came over the fax machine is a day Margulies will never forget.[69]

In that dissent, Justice Blackmun, who struggled to enforce the death penalty on the bench for more than twenty years, suddenly announced, "From this day forward I no longer shall tinker with the machinery of death." Despite judicial efforts to ensure death sentences were "imposed fairly, and with reasonable consistency, or not at all," Blackmun wrote, he concluded at the twilight of his career that "the death penalty remains fraught with arbitrariness, discrimination, caprice, and mistake." "Even under the most sophisticated death penalty statutes," Blackmun lamented, "race continues to play a major role in determining who shall live and who shall die." That judgment, Blackmun wrote, objecting to the Court's refusal even to hear the case of Bruce Callins, who murdered a man in a Texas tavern, "is so inherently subjective—rife with all of life's understandings, experiences, prejudices, and passions—that it inevitably defies the rationality and consistency required by the Constitution." At Callins's trial, a venireman revealed during voir dire that a fellow venire member had called Callins a "nigger" and speculated as to how he could afford to pay for legal counsel. Callins moved for a mistrial, but the trial court denied that motion, and the Fifth Circuit let the conviction stand, ruling that no "prejudice" resulted from the racist remark.[70]

In his dissent, calling the criminal justice system "less than perfect" and saying "human error" and "factual, legal, and moral error" is "inevitable," Blackmun, long troubled by America's death penalty, found it unconstitutional just before his retirement. "The path the Court has chosen lessens us all," he said, chiding his fellow justices for deciding "to deregulate" America's death penalty by failing to provide "meaningful judicial oversight" over death sentences. After watching it operate, Blackmun simply refused to participate any longer in a system that strapped people to a gurney and used "intravenous tubes" and "toxic fluid designed specifically for the purpose of killing human beings." "I feel morally and intellectually obligated simply to concede that the death penalty experiment has failed," he said in dissent.[71]

SIX

Men in Black

Jim Willett, an ex-warden at Huntsville's prison, oversaw eighty-nine Texas executions in three years. Joseph Cannon's was the first one. After the "tie-down" crew strapped Cannon to the gurney, an IV was inserted, then fell out. Willett closed the curtains, and the IV was reinserted out of the presence of the witnesses. The execution then resumed. "I took off my glasses," Willett recounted after retiring. "That was the signal to the hidden executioner to start the flow of the three fluids, one to put him to sleep, one to collapse his lungs and diaphragm, one to stop his heart. I waited three minutes before asking the doctor to make his pronouncement. Then I went home to my family." "It was the most emotionally draining experience I'd ever had," he recalled later. "It would get easier with routine," Willett said. "But it would never get easy."[1]

Being an executioner is hard to imagine, and only a handful of people know the personal toll that job can take. "Sometimes I wonder whether people really understand what goes on down here and the effect it has on us," Jim Willett asks himself. "Some people, they might like to drink and, you know, forget about it," says Kenneth Dean of the Huntsville unit. "I like the outdoors," he adds, "and that's just how I cope with it." His colleague, Fred Allen, actually broke down in 1998 after taking part in 130 executions as part of Huntsville's tie-down team. "I was just working in the shop and all of the sudden something just triggered in me, and I started shaking," Allen remembers. When he told his wife, "I don't feel so good," she asked her husband, who was crying uncontrollably, "What's the matter?" "I just thought about that execution that I did two days ago, and everybody else's that I was involved in," he confided to her. Fred Allen now works as a carpenter. "Lots of guards quit," a prison chaplain admits.[2]

"People wonder how I could do it," Jim Willett says. "I remind them that mine was but the final contribution to a long, complex process," he explains. "Each juror had a part, along with the attorneys and witnesses and judges." "I walked out of this job much the same as when I began it," Willett reflected, "full of questions" and "with a gnawing in my gut that hasn't gone away." He knows the system is flawed, and he holds no illusions about what that means. "Has an innocent man ever been executed?" Willett asks. "Probably," he answers. "Anyone who expects perfection is asking for an impossibility." Willett's most vivid memories of his work in Texas's death house are of watching convicted killers' relatives on execution day. "A new set of victims is created among the family members of the condemned who watch," Willett laments. "I wondered most about the mothers who saw their sons being put to death," he says. "Some would just wail out crying. It's a sound you'll never hear any place else, an awful sound that sticks with you."[3]

Though prison officials in Utah and other states have resorted to setting up stress inoculation programs or offering counseling for execution participants, politicians often say they support capital punishment because the public wants it. When Governor George Pataki fulfilled a campaign pledge to bring back New York's death penalty, he said that "the overwhelming majority of voters" demanded it. Calling government "an instrument of the people," Pataki emphasized that "legislation must reflect the will of those who entrust representatives to create the laws of society." Others say much the same thing. "I'm going to uphold the law of the land and let the political consequences be what they may," Texas Governor George W. Bush said while on the presidential campaign trail. "The reason I support the death penalty is because it saves lives. That's why I support it, and the people of my state support it too."[4]

Such statements, which presume a groundswell of support for capital punishment, are based, at least in part, on flawed public opinion polls. More than two-thirds of Americans say they "favor" death sentences when asked the oversimplified question "Do you favor or oppose the death penalty for persons convicted of murder?" Yet, when asked to choose between the death penalty and life without parole, support for the death penalty drops sharply—by at least 15–20 percent, and even more dramatically in some polls. In an ABC News poll taken in October 2000, the percentage of those expressing support for capital punishment fell to 48 percent when life without parole was given as an option. Death penalty support drops even further if pollsters add the condition that murderers be required to work in prison to earn money to pay restitution to victims' families.[5]

The death penalty's morality, of course, cannot be assessed by looking at public opinion polls. What these polls show, however, is that support for capital punishment is actually quite shallow. A Gallup poll done in 2002 found that 40 percent of respondents think the death penalty is applied unfairly, and another ABC News poll conducted in 2001 found that 51 percent of Americans support a nationwide moratorium on executions. Other polls show that a majority of Americans oppose the execution of the mentally ill and would not want to pull the switch at executions themselves. These latter polls confirm just how ambivalent Americans feel about the death penalty and how, in reality, many Americans prefer a tough, effective alternative to it: life in prison without any possibility of release.[6]

The public's lack of exposure to executions may explain these polling variations. American laws universally outlaw public executions, and no state permits television cameras to film them. As a result, for all but a few official witnesses and prison guards, executions are mere abstractions; to most of the public, executions are shrouded in secrecy and they are hidden from public view. Indeed, to further reduce media exposure, executions are often conducted in the dead of night. Between 1977 and 1995, over 80 percent of the 313 executions that took place in the United States happened between 11:00 P.M. and 7:00 A.M.; over 50 percent of them occurred between midnight and 1:00 A.M.[7]

After-dark executions are a deliberate choice by lawmakers or prison officials and are often mandated by statute. Delaware and Louisiana require executions between midnight and 3:00 A.M., and Wyoming and Indiana mandate executions "before the hour of sunrise." Only recently did Texas change its practice of scheduling executions for one minute after midnight; in that state, executions are now conducted shortly after 6:00 P.M. so judges no longer need to be awakened in the middle of the night to decide a man's—or, in rare instances, a woman's—fate.[8]

The exclusion of television cameras from executions and the practice of conducting them under cover of darkness have only contributed to the public's apathy. At Clifton Belyeu's execution, Larry Fitzgerald, the spokesman for the Texas Department of Criminal Justice, reported that only two or three protestors showed up at the Huntsville prison. "Of course, that was a Friday," Fitzgerald said. "Maybe it was Miller Time for everybody. But there was hardly anybody there."[9]

The low turnout is largely attributable to the fact that executions are now routine—there were thirty-seven in Texas in 1997 alone—and that many of them simply are not publicized anymore. The first execution in twenty-five years in a state, as was the case with California's 1992 execution of Robert Alton Harris, may draw hordes of reporters and spark well-attended candlelight vigils. But with each passing execution, there is less and less media and public interest.[10]

The ban on television cameras from execution chambers has, in fact, taken away two of abolitionists' most powerful arguments: the faces of execution participants and condemned inmates and the public's ability to see for themselves the violent act, however sanitized, of the execution itself. Because of the lack of television coverage, death row inmates, already dehumanized in capital trials, are perceived as unseen monsters or ugly mug shots, not as fellow human beings, however depraved, with parents, siblings, and children like the rest of us.

The case of Karla Faye Tucker—the first woman executed in Texas since the Civil War—showed just how powerful a human face can be. After widely publicized pleas for mercy, coming from religious leaders as diverse as Pope John Paul II and Pat Robertson, a Texas poll found that only 48 percent of Texans wanted the execution to go forward, even though another poll showed 75 percent of state residents favored capital punishment in the abstract. That executions are conducted out of the public eye means that Americans are never forced to watch what the government is doing on their behalf.[11]

American politicians who work for the death penalty's abolition have become an endangered—at times, almost extinct—species. After the Oklahoma City bombing, the U.S. Senate voted unanimously—without a single dissenting vote—that a jury should be allowed to sentence to death any perpetrator of the bombing. While a large and growing number of politicians are supportive of a moratorium on executions, only a few politicians, such as Senator Russ Feingold and Congressman Jesse Jackson, Jr., have spent considerable time on efforts aimed at repealing death penalty laws.[12]

Both Democrats and Republicans alike frequently love to tout their support for capital punishment. In the thick of the crucial New Hampshire primary in the 1992 presidential election, Bill Clinton, embroiled in the sex scandal involving Gennifer Flowers, flew back to Little Rock, Arkansas, to oversee the execution of Rickey Ray Rector. Rector had killed a police officer, then shot himself in the head, causing severe brain damage. On the day of his execution, Rector actually tried to save a slice of pecan pie from his last meal, believing he would be back for dessert after the execution.[13]

As governor of Texas, George W. Bush refused to speak out against the execution of Karla Faye Tucker, even though pleas for clemency poured into Texas from around the world. Indeed, as the Republican presidential candidate, Bush mocked the attempt of Karla Faye Tucker to obtain executive clemency. "Please don't kill me," Bush imitated Tucker in a whimpering tone. The Bush Administration's Justice Department continues to seek death sentences in criminal cases, with Attorney General John Ashcroft having overruled his own prosecutors at least sixteen times when they did not recommend death penalty charges, and as commander-in-chief, Bush has signed orders allowing military tribunals to impose death sentences.[14]

The late Justice Thurgood Marshall once wrote that Americans, if "fully informed as to the purposes of the death penalty and its liabilities," would "reject it as morally unacceptable."[15] I agree.

A public armed with full information and continually confronted with televised images of executions on CNN and the nightly news would be sickened by state-sanctioned killing. As it stands now, though, the public—which gets much of its news from television—gets little information about executions and so naturally focuses its attention elsewhere. Of the ninety-three executions between 1977 and 1987, only thirty-three received network news coverage. As a result of the paucity of television reports exposing these spectacles, television reporters and newspaper editorial boards rarely ask politicians hard-hitting questions about the death penalty. Because elected officials are never forced to explain how state-sanctioned violence can somehow reduce violence, the dead bodies just keep piling up.[16]

Make no mistake: convicted killers belong behind bars. Men like Clifton Belyeu and death row escapee Martin Gurule were found by juries to have participated in violent, lethal robberies, and prison is where both men belonged for their crimes. By robbing and killing, a convicted felon forfeits the right to walk our sidewalks and streets and to roam our parks and neighborhoods. Justice requires that murderers be held accountable for their actions and that violent offenders be incarcerated to protect law-abiding citizens.[17]

Over a decade ago, convicted murderers spent, on average, less than seven years behind bars. That catch-and-release policy for violent offenders—which some Americans still perceive exists today—was totally unacceptable, as state legislatures across the country soon realized.[18]

Fortunately, of the thirty-eight states that now authorize capital punishment, thirty-five provide life without parole as a sentencing option, with the remaining states guaranteeing long prison terms—up to forty years, for example—before convicted killers are eligible for parole. The remaining states, Kansas, New Mexico, and Texas, which fail to authorize life-without-parole sentences for murder, must do so at once.[19]

It is unconscionable that some juries continue to be faced with the Hobson's choice of imposing death sentences or voting for sentences that are too lenient. Jurors should never be forced to vote for death out of a belief that, if they do not, a heinous killer might be allowed to walk the streets again. Americans deserve truth in sentencing so that a "life" sentence means a life sentence, and judges and jurors must always have life without parole as a sentencing option. Prisoners must be treated humanely, but maximum-security prisons, with strict rules to ensure the safety of guards and others, are where violent offenders belong.[20]

Executing people in cold blood behind thick prison walls, by contrast, does no good; secretive, nighttime executions merely demonstrate how ashamed we are of what our own government is doing. Only in dictatorships or places such as Japan, where inmates spend up to thirty years on death row before being executed, are executions conducted more secretly. Condemned inmates' families in Japan are not notified of executions until after they occur, and prisoners themselves may receive only one hour's notice before they are taken to a room with a small Buddhist altar, given a last meal, blindfolded, and then hanged. The executions are usually conducted when Japan's Parliament is in recess, and the Japanese Ministry of Justice refuses to release even the names of those executed, except to relatives.[21]

Indeed, state-sanctioned executions do damage only to ourselves. They tarnish our respect for human life and institutionalize killing, all the while posing the ever-present risk of fatal mistakes. We rightfully express outrage at terrorist attacks, school and drive-by shootings, and acts of workplace and domestic violence. Yet, by allowing state-sanctioned killings, a deliberate and calculated form of violence, we allow our tax dollars to be used to inject even more violence into our society, all right inside government-owned buildings. By averting our eyes from executions, we allow the death penalty machinery to churn on with our tacit approval.

Ironically, while American politicians who trumpet capital punishment are routinely rewarded at the polls with election and reelection, executioners—who actually carry out death sentences—have been shunned throughout history. In the heyday of public executions in France, executioners' houses were painted red, and executioners' daughters were forbidden to marry men outside their fathers' profession. Modern-day Florida executioners still wear black hoods to protect their identities, and Illinois executioners have been paid in cash for their services so that no paper trail of their gruesome work exists. When Charles Campbell went to the gallows shortly after midnight in the state of Washington in 1994, the executioner's identity was masked by blinds, which allowed official witnesses to see only his silhouette.[22]

I myself have never understood why executioners are treated as social outcasts, even as those who sign death warrants or pass death penalty laws are held up as role models. Don't executioners and those who facilitate death sentences have more in common than we have allowed ourselves to acknowledge? After all, without judges, jurors, and politicians, the executioners would be doing other, more productive work. While executioners may follow orders, it is governors and lawmakers, trying to prove how "tough" they are on crime, who make executions possible, and it is jurors' and judges' pen strokes that seal prisoners' fates. Perhaps if politicians, judges, and jurors were forced to pull the switch at executions they voted for, they wouldn't be so quick to condemn human beings to die in the first place.

The secrecy surrounding executions, of course, runs completely contrary to modern American ideals of accountability and openness in government, of which open-meeting laws and the Freedom of Information Act are just two examples. Although legislators and judges have so far managed to keep executions off television—rejecting bills to broadcast them and journalists' lawsuits seeking to film them—the result has been only to lessen the availability of public information surrounding them.[23]

Many judges find the death penalty immoral or have deep, personal misgivings about its use. Yet, by rejecting broadcasters' lawsuits in states such as California, North Carolina, and Texas seeking to film executions, it is judges themselves—fearful of the prospect of television coverage—who have prevented the public from learning about the cold, inhumane reality of these judicially sanctioned acts. Appalled at the idea of television coverage of the U.S. Supreme Court's own oral arguments, Justice David Souter—expressing judges' paranoia toward television—once told legislators, "The day you see a camera coming into our courtroom, it's going to roll over my dead body."[24]

America's death penalty machinery, meanwhile, is designed and engineered as a kind of shell game of moral responsibility. Legislators just vote for death penalty statutes; it is prosecutors who seek death sentences and trial judges and jurors who impose them. Prosecutors, judges, and jurors don't make the law, they just enforce it, and appellate judges just review death sentences already imposed by others. Governors, who possess clemency powers but hardly ever use them, sidestep personal responsibility for executions too by simply deferring to judicial determinations. Only one death sentence was commuted in 1994, and no clemency petitions for death row inmates were granted at all in 1995. From 1976 to 2002, only forty-nine death row inmates had their death sentences commuted to prison terms for humanitarian reasons through the use of executive clemency. Governor Edwin Edwards of Louisiana went so far as to transfer the responsibility of signing death warrants from himself to the sentencing judge to further distance himself from death's machinery. While at least one death row inmate has been granted clemency in every year since 1996, many governors—with the notable exception of Governor George Ryan, who emptied Illinois's death row—continue to be extremely reluctant to set aside death sentences.[25]

Right now, elected officials, judges, and jurors are not even required to attend executions, as they were in New York in the 1840s, much less pull the switch at them. Instead, anonymous executioners do the dirty work while the rest of us slumber or eat dinner after work. Even executioners, torn up as they are by their role at executions, are supposed to be allowed to leave execution chambers without feeling any personal guilt. A blank is put in one of five firing squad guns, or only one of two buttons—pushed by different individuals—activates the lethal injection machine. Executioners are not morally responsible for their actions, they are told; they are just doing their jobs. Even the clinical way we typically put people to death these days—lethal injection—is intended to sanitize the fact that we are killing someone.[26]

A recent decision of the U.S. Court of Appeals for the Ninth Circuit illustrates the system's total lack of personal accountability for death sentences. In that case, David Lewis Rice, a criminal defendant, was absent from the courtroom when the jury sentenced him to die. Before the jury finished deliberating, the judge learned that Rice had been hospitalized after ingesting a nicotine drink brewed from cigarettes. Medical personnel told the judge that Rice was unresponsive and had to have his stomach pumped. Instead of waiting for Rice's return, the state trial judge simply proceeded with his sentencing. The jury sentenced Rice to die without even looking into his eyes at the moment the verdict was read.[27]

In its 1996 opinion written by Judge Alex Kozinski, the Ninth Circuit upheld Rice's death sentence. Rice's absence when the jury sentenced him to death was described as "trivial" and "harmless error." Kozinski discounted the possibility that the jury, when polled and forced to look at Rice, might have had a change in heart. A vigorous dissent chided Kozinski's ruling as "the ultimate triumph of procedure over substance: the person is now irrelevant to the process." Referring to the writings of Franz Kafka and one of the novelist's characters, the dissent wrote: "This is the nightmare world of *The Trial*; it is not American justice. Like Josef K, David Lewis Rice was sentenced to death in absentia, and, like Josef K, Rice will go to his grave asking, 'Where is the judge whom I have never seen?' "[28]

Any death penalty opponent, of course, must confront head-on the most horrendous of cases, like that of the Oklahoma City bomber Timothy McVeigh. Such cases often involve little or no question of guilt; the person has confessed to the crime, overwhelming evidence corroborates the confession, and the only question is what punishment should be imposed. McVeigh, a Gulf War veteran obsessed with the government's 1993 siege of the Branch Davidian complex, freely admitted his guilt as his execution approached. "The truth is, I blew up the Murrah building," the remorseless McVeigh said of his terrorist act, almost bragging about it. Referring to the nineteen children killed in the attack as "collateral damage," McVeigh regretted only that their deaths had distracted from his asserted motive: to avenge what McVeigh saw as governmental abuses of power. When McVeigh's father, Bill McVeigh, asked his only son why he did it, he said "Dad, it all came down to Waco."[29]

Many people saw Timothy McVeigh as the poster boy for the death penalty, and they got their way: he was executed. The pain of survivors of the tragedy and victims' families was palpable, even far from Oklahoma City. Three survivors and seven bombing victims' relatives were selected by lottery to sit in Terre Haute's federal execution chamber to watch McVeigh die. One of those relatives, Kay Fulton, was from Red Wing, Minnesota, not far from where I live. As deadly chemicals flowed into McVeigh's body, Fulton pressed a photograph of her brother, Paul Ice, up against the death chamber's window, even though McVeigh couldn't see through the one-way glass. Ice, a forty-two-year-old customs agent, had died in the bombing. "Symbolically, I felt it was a way for Paul to watch his murderer die," Fulton told reporters after the execution.[30]

All McVeigh's execution really did, though, was cap off a life filled with hate with a final retaliatory act of rage and deprive another set of already grief-stricken parents of a son. When asked if he had forgiven his son for bombing the Alfred P. Murrah Federal Building, Bill McVeigh replied, "That's a tough one." An army veteran who worked on the assembly line for the United Automobile Workers for twenty-five years, Bill McVeigh despised what his son had done, yet still felt his son should live. "How can you forgive him for killing 168 people?" Bill McVeigh said of his son's terrorist act, carried out with a three- to six-thousand-pound ammonium-nitrate bomb carried inside a Ryder truck. "You can't. He's my son, but he did something that was terribly wrong." "I wouldn't have any idea why he would do something like that," Bill McVeigh said. "It still baffles me."[31]

Bud Welch, whose only daughter was killed in the blast, was one of the few people who spoke out against McVeigh's execution. "The day Timothy McVeigh is taken from that cage in Indiana and put to death is not going to bring Julie Marie Welch back and is not going to bring me any peace or anybody in this nation any peace," he said. "God did not make us so that we feel good about killing a caged human being." For months after his twenty-three-year-old daughter died in the bombing, Bud Welch, a Texaco service station owner, felt only rage, depression, and grief. "I didn't even want trials for them," Welch said of Timothy McVeigh and his codefendant, Terry Nichols. "I wanted them fried." After smoking three packs of cigarettes a day and drinking himself to sleep at night, Welch, realizing his life was falling apart, finally abandoned thoughts of revenge, let go of his rage, and arranged to visit Bill McVeigh at his home near Buffalo, New York. "The reason Julie and 167 others were dead was rage and revenge," Bud Welch would say before Timothy McVeigh's execution.[32]

On my way back from a friend's wedding in Florida, I remember watching television in a crowded airport as news of Timothy McVeigh's case—in particular, the federal government's late disclosure of documents to the defense—dominated the headlines. With children sitting next to me, I thought to myself about the questions children must be asking their parents and themselves. If Timothy McVeigh—a pathetic soul who sought martyrdom for his twisted cause—had just been sent to prison, America's children would not be forced to hear high-level government officials such as U.S. Attorney General John Ashcroft talk of meticulously planned executions. Why couldn't we just have sent McVeigh to prison for the rest of his natural life like other mentally deranged killers such as the Unabomber?

Executions are "something I won't miss a bit," Texas warden Jim Willett said a year before his retirement. "You know," he reflected even then, "there are times when I'm standing there, watching those fluids start to flow, and wonder whether what we're doing here is right. It's something I'll think about for the rest of my life." "It's hard explaining to a seven-year-old," Kenneth Dean adds, talking about his role as head of the tie-down team and his own daughter's probing questions: "What is an execution? What do you do?" A Baptist, Dean prays before and after every execution. "All of us wonder if it's right," he says. "If jurors had to draw straws to see who was going to pull the switch or start the lethal injection," Willett concludes, "there wouldn't be as many executions."[33]

It's high time for all of us, as Americans, to own up to our own role in executions. That means, in simple English, that we must stop looking away from state-sanctioned killing and ask some tough questions. Is what we're doing right? Or is it immoral and totally at odds with our own value system? It means, in very practical terms, that if politicians continue to allow executions to be carried out, television cameras must be allowed into execution chambers so that the electorate can see and hear for themselves what they are allowing to happen. The First Amendment and the freedom of the press—not to mention America's commitment to openness in government—demand no less.[34]

Print and broadcast journalists alike must be allowed to report fully on the innermost workings of government, be they in the U.S. Senate, the federal courts, or lethal execution chambers. Only if Americans are allowed to see for themselves the tragic consequences of the death penalty in action will they be better able to judge for themselves its morality.

A death penalty supporter, Judge Kozinski himself loses sleep and expresses "a nagging sense of unease, something like motion sickness," for playing a part in ending the lives of death row inmates. Writing in the *New Yorker*, Kozinski recounted a conversation with Bill Allen, a former law firm colleague, whose death row client, Linwood Briley, had just been executed. "The look on Bill's face stayed with me a long time," Kozinski wrote. "It was enough to persuade me that I'd never want to witness an execution."[35]

Even Judge Kozinski, who regularly allows executions, says it "bothers" him that, in using lethal injections, "we mask the most violent act that society can inflict on one of its members with such an antiseptic veneer." And Kozinski, asking whether capital punishment "is not an expensive and distracting sideshow to our battle against violent crime," freely expresses a little self-doubt: "I sometimes wonder whether those of us who make life-and-death decisions on a regular basis should not be required to watch as the machinery of death grinds up a human being." "I ponder what it says about me," Kozinski says, "that I can, with cool precision, cast votes and write opinions that seal another human being's fate but lack the courage to witness the consequences of my actions."[36]

Maybe it's finally time for all of us—including Judge Kozinski, who metes out justice in his long black robe—to watch up close as, with each passing execution, America tops off an already violent society with yet another violent act. Perhaps Judge Kozinski and the rest of us should get to know Fred Allen, the Texan who broke down after participating in more than a hundred executions. "There were so many," Allen remembers in a trembling voice. "A lot of this stuff I just want to forget." Fred Allen does not sit in the White House, but he has been forever changed by what he saw. He, like Bud Welch, had an epiphany after enduring so much pain and suffering. "There's nothing wrong," Allen says now, "with an individual spending the rest of his life in prison."[37]

A lot of people get queasy over the prospect of televised executions. I myself shudder at the thought of watching one. But if you think about it, is it television or the executions themselves

that make us so uneasy? After all, we see lots of things on TV—
nonviolent PBS specials, for one—that don't disturb us. Cameras
merely capture on film what actors or ordinary people do; it is the
words and actions of those being filmed that influence our emo-
tional response to a given event and that determine, for example,
whether a movie is rated X, R, PG, or G. It must be what happens
at executions, then, not the presence of cameras in the execution
chambers, that offends our collective sensibilities. Indeed, in this
age of rampant TV violence, it's more than a bit strange that
state-sanctioned violence is the only form of violence not on television. Executions are certainly newsworthy events, and in a
country that cherishes the freedom of the press, it's unclear why
politicians have been allowed to hide executions from public
view and sanitize the news for so long. If we aren't willing to
watch executions, we shouldn't have them in the first place.

Will putting executions on television lead to the abolition of
capital punishment? It's hard to say, really. Certainly, skeptics
abound. Showing executions on television may only increase support for the death penalty, some say. People are too desensitized
to violence on television for televised executions to change minds,
others insist.

There is no way to predict, but the skeptics may be wrong. Televised executions might well spell the quick demise of America's
death penalty, just as the tawdry violence of public executions decades ago led to moving them into prisons at the dead of night.

Why might this happen? It's simple: people know the difference
between real violence and film-and-TV "entertainment" violence, and they react differently to them. Film clips of Vietnam ig-
nited the antiwar movement, and the Rodney King video outraged
television viewers and sparked a nationwide debate about police
brutality. Moviegoers may shrug off the violence seen in James
Bond or Arnold Schwarzenegger films, but they react with horror
when they see real human suffering, be it in Bosnia, the Middle
East, or in their own hometowns.[38]

The amount of violence on television already is staggering. By

age eighteen, the average teenager has seen forty thousand drama-
tized murders. But just because violent programming may be offensive or disturbing does not mean that film footage of executions or
other violent acts—whether simulated or real—should be censored.
Parents must, of course, monitor what their kids watch at home
and on the big screen, but television stations and filmmakers
have—as they should—the right to portray acts of violence.[39]

Though sometimes sensationalized, many hard-hitting TV
news stories have exposed real problems—child abuse and domestic violence, to name just two—that deserve our attention, and
sometimes depictions of violence can be a call to action as much
as gratuitous portrayals. Films such as *Schindler's List* and *Saving Private Ryan*, while depicting violence, were responsibly produced to convey the horror of it. If Americans saw executions, I
believe, as Sister Helen Prejean does, they would be repelled by
them.[40]

Media representatives, in fact, have an ethical obligation to ex-
pose violence in its many forms. For only if Americans are made
aware of violence can they take action to eradicate it, whether by
passing tougher gun or child protection laws or pushing for longer
prison sentences for violent offenders.

If executions were televised, the American public would see
the faces of men like Clifton Belyeu and our role in executions
would become inescapable and undeniable. We would be forced to
ask ourselves some disturbing questions. What, if anything, do we
accomplish by putting people to death? Are we only worsening
the problem of violence in our society? And do we ourselves
really occupy any position different from that of paid, professional
executioners, who themselves are uneasy about what they are being asked to do?

After all, in a democracy, it is the people themselves who send
pro–death penalty politicians to Washington, D.C., and to our
statehouses. If Americans stopped oiling the machinery of death,
the executioners could go back to being wardens and prison

guards without the burden of having to kill people as part of their jobs.

As a lawyer, I see the death penalty as having only a corrosive influence on the development of the law. The legal system can do much that is good, but capital punishment laws don't stop violence, they just promote it. Using the law to kill incarcerated criminals is not only pathetic but wrong. All the death penalty really does is require judges in black robes—some of the best and brightest minds our country has to offer—to spend vast amounts of their time deciding whether mostly poor, mentally disturbed defendants should live or die.

If U.S. senators, state legislators, or members of the U.S. Supreme Court had to push the buttons that activate lethal injection machines, I wonder whether Americans would feel the same way about them? I doubt it. Only because responsibility for executions is spread so diffusely among the various actors in the criminal justice system do judges and jurors feel permission to disavow responsibility for the sentences they impose.[41]

With every execution, the cycle of murder and hate—like a shoot-out between the Hatfields and the McCoys—repeats itself. At a botched electrocution in Florida, flames leaped from the head of the convicted killer Pedro Medina as the electric chair malfunctioned, leaving the stench of burning flesh lingering in the air. Seven months later, a divided Florida Supreme Court— clearing the way for more executions—brushed the incident aside, ruling that electrocution is not cruel or unusual punishment. Only after a dissenting judge posted photographs on the Internet showing the bloody, contorted face of an electrocuted man, did the U.S. Supreme Court halt a Florida electrocution and even agree to consider—as it did nearly a century ago—the constitutionality of electrocution as a means of killing.[42]

In Jasper, Texas, James Byrd, a black man walking home from a party, was kidnapped and tied to a truck with a twenty-four-foot logging chain and dragged alive on asphalt for almost three miles

until he was decapitated and dismembered. One of the perpetrators, Shawn Allen Berry, got a "life" sentence for his role in the
crime, which in Texas means he must spend forty years behind
bars before he can be considered for parole. The other two convicted killers, however, were sentenced to die. John William King
and Lawrence Russell Brewer, both white supremacists, tattooed
with satanic stars and Nazi and racist symbols, were shipped after
their sentencing proceedings to Huntsville's James Byrd Diagnos-
tic Unit, named for an ex-warden, not the murder victim. Although
James Byrd's only son, Ross Byrd, has protested the execution of
his father's killers, King and Brewer still sit on death row. The
thirst for blood, the hate that fuels racism and revenge, is seem-
ingly never quenched.[43]

Epilogue

I grew up in a family in which I was taught to respect life; my mother and father raised six boys and created a secure, loving environment for all of us. I never went hungry, I had swimming and piano lessons, and they made sure I got a quality education. They read books to us at bedtime, did lots of community volunteer work, and bought us clothes and pencils and spiral notebooks with each new school year. My dad, a biologist, has devoted his career to the study of living things. He let us peer through microscopes at Mankato State University, and on summer camping trips to Yellowstone, the Smoky Mountains, and Yosemite National Park, we identified trees and wildflowers together as we grew closer as a family.

Those on death row, by contrast, are almost always the product of highly dysfunctional, violence-prone families, and their childhoods are often marked by head trauma, severe verbal and physical abuse, drug addiction or alcoholism, or some combination thereof. Dr. Dorothy Otnow Lewis, a New York University psychiatrist, studied fifteen adults on death row and found all of them had suffered severe head injuries—corroborated by cranium indentations, hospital records, scars, or CAT scans—and that twelve of them had neurological problems. Another study of fourteen juveniles on death row, done by Lewis and Georgetown University neurologist Jonathan Pincus, found that all fourteen had suffered serious head injuries, that twelve of fourteen were severely beaten, and that five had been sexually molested. The study of fifteen death row inmates found a total of forty-eight significant head injuries in those inmates alone. The medical notations these researchers reviewed make it fairly easy to see how violent criminals are born.[1]

I recently read a new book by Pulitzer Prize–winning author, Richard Rhodes, called *Why They Kill*, which helps explain—perhaps as much as we can ever know—why violent acts are committed. In it, Rhodes tells the story of Dr. Lonnie Athens, a criminologist. Savagely abused as a child by his own father, Athens has spent his time in academia studying the origins of violent behavior. He has conducted scores of lengthy interviews with murderers, rapists, and other violent offenders to try to understand why some people murder, rape, and commit vicious assaults. What Athens has found, in case after case, is what he calls a "violentization" process, a phrase he coined to describe the socialization mechanism that creates violent criminals. The findings of Athens's research are as chilling as they should be compelling to anyone who has even a little common sense.[2]

The violentization process, Athens explains, has four stages: brutalization, belligerency, violent performances, and virulency. The first stage—brutalization—is composed mainly of violent subjugation, in which authority figures such as parents or gang leaders use or threaten violence until the subject of it signals submission, and violent coaching, whereby a person is taught to use violence in interacting with others. The result of this coaching and continual abuse, intimidation, and humiliation is a sense of helplessness and worthlessness that leads abused individuals to become belligerent to try to stop the abuse. If a subject's violent reactions to abuse—what Athens calls "violent performances"— end in draws or defeats, the abused individual may abandon violence altogether or, paradoxically, decide to resort more quickly to more lethal forms of it. If the subject prevails in violent encounters, however, the person is emboldened and feels powerful, perhaps for the first time. Now virulent, he is ready, willing, and able to inflict violence upon others, often without provocation. "He has now gone full circle," Athens says, "from a hapless victim of brutalization to a ruthless aggressor—the same kind of brutalizer whom he had earlier despised."[3]

The vicious cycle of violence that Athens describes may, at times, seem like an intractable problem, but it is not. Child protection workers, armed with this knowledge, can remove abused and neglected children from homes, and effective, one-on-one mentoring programs like Big Brothers/Big Sisters can be expanded to provide positive role models to counterbalance negative influences in children's lives. A 1995 study of that program showed that mentored youth were 46 percent less likely to begin using drugs, 27 percent less likely to begin drinking, and 33 percent less likely to hit someone. Schools, too, can make a big difference. When researchers tracked nine hundred children from some of Chicago's poorest neighborhoods, they found that schoolchildren who had attended Head Start–like preschool programs had juvenile arrest rates 33 percent lower than those who had not; the study group's violent crime rate was 41 percent lower, and high school graduation rates were higher. "Although the community cannot guarantee a good family to every child," Athens says, "it can guarantee them a good school," which "can go a long way in making up for a bad family."[4]

For years now, I've followed America's death penalty debate, much as Athens has tracked the lives of violent offenders. As a teacher, I've trained law students to handle capital litigation; as a concerned citizen, I've testified against the death penalty's reinstatement in my home state; and at my writing desk, I've read scores of newspaper and magazine articles about murders and executions. What I've been struck by again and again is how often death row inmates' lives fit the pattern of abuse and criminality that Athens and medical professionals like Dr. Pincus describe in their own writings on the subject of violent behavior. Having examined roughly 150 murderers, Pincus has repeatedly seen grotesque sexual and physical abuse in the backgrounds of serial killers and other murderers, frequently coupled with mental illness, paranoia, and brain damage inflicted at the hands of their abusers.[5]

Like nearly everyone, I suspect, I know people who favor capital punishment, those who oppose it, and those who simply haven't made up their minds. My students, friends, and neighbors hold widely divergent views, though most people I have talked to are at least ambivalent about some aspect of the death penalty. They worry about the execution of juveniles, the innocent, or the mentally ill, or they worry that the criminal justice system is racially discriminatory, arbitrary, or unfair in its application. In short, there is room for movement in America's death penalty debate and for minds to be changed. Recent polls showing considerable support for a moratorium on executions, along with a number of public hearings and legislative bills on that subject, show just how receptive at least some Americans have become to change.[6]

If the anti–death penalty movement is to succeed, it must first overcome the apathy that exists among a large segment of the American public. Capital punishment affects the lives of judges and jurors, prosecutors and public defenders, prison guards and executioners, and, of course, convicted killers. However, for the vast majority of voters, the death penalty is simply not an issue that affects their day-to-day lives; if a murderer is executed, their lives go on just the same. Although capital punishment is likely to be abolished at some point in the future even without televised executions, putting executions on television will get the public's attention more quickly. Even if judges and policymakers never permit them, just the thought of such spectacles should help force people to think about capital punishment in a different light.

Once the public is listening, anti–death penalty advocates must make sure that life-without-parole sentences are a sentencing option for convicted killers. Until places like Texas give jurors the right to impose such sentences, juries will continue to vote for death sentences over legitimate worries that dangerous, convicted killers will one day be set free. The public has a right to be protected from violent offenders, and life-without-parole sentences strike the appropriate balance between the need for public safety and the need to be tough on violence that doing away with capital punishment requires.

The September 11th terrorist attacks have led, in some quarters, to public cries for the death penalty's use against terrorists and renewed calls for the execution of murderers. It would be a tragic mistake, however, to let a terrorist attack stymie America's abolitionist movement or silence the voices of those who have spoken out so forcefully against death as a form of punishment. The death penalty's problems—the conviction of the innocent, racial discrimination in its application, and the abysmal quality of counsel at so many capital trials—are legion, and this reality certainly has not changed since September 11th. Indeed, no past or future crime or terrorist attack will alter those cold, hard facts.

At this turbulent time in the world's history, the threats of violence we face are real and cannot be underestimated. There are the global threats of chemical, biological, and nuclear weapons; there are terrorists, right-wing militia, and paramilitary groups; and there are religious fanatics and white supremacists. Sex offenders and felons with guns live in our cities and townships, and in foreign countries, terrorist camps continue to operate, and thousands of unexploded land mines lie just beneath the surface of the earth waiting to claim more lives and limbs. The squalid and oppressive poverty that exists in so many parts of the world serves as a dangerous incubator, I'm afraid, for future terrorists and murderers.

Now more than ever, Americans must do everything we can to eradicate all forms of violence. The war against terrorism must be fought, for future attacks must be thwarted and it is unjust to allow terrorists—however mentally deranged or distant from American soil—to escape the consequences of their actions. However, instead of spending our time and resources executing people, we need to channel our efforts into more productive endeavors, such as improving the quality of schools, fighting poverty and child abuse, and better regulating firearms to reduce gun violence. Firearm death rates in Asia are nearly one hundred times lower than in the Americas, and violence, while difficult to predict or stop, is a global health problem that we urgently need to take steps to eradicate. At a recent World Health Organization conference, one doctor, Etienne Krug, put it succinctly: "Regional differences in homicide and firearm death rates suggest . . . that much violence is preventable."[7]

Individual citizens can make a difference. Sarah Brady, whose husband was shot and disabled during the assassination attempt on Ronald Reagan, fought for passage of the Brady Bill in Congress. Background checks under that law have stopped nearly 700,000 felons and other legally prohibited gun buyers from acquiring guns from licensed dealers. Another woman, Donna Dees-Thomases, moved by images of children after a white supremacist opened fire at a Jewish community center in California, started the Million Mom March for mothers to go to Washington, D.C., on Mother's Day to demand tougher gun laws. In 2000, more than 750,000 people marched on the Mall in the nation's capital to demonstrate their support for such laws. And Sister Helen Prejean's work has, all by itself, transformed America's death penalty debate.[8]

While taking action on the home front, Americans must also look outward and help those most in need in underdeveloped countries. A United Nations report shows that 2.8 of the world's 6 billion people live on less than two dollars a day, and in places as diverse as Africa, Asia, and Latin America, people are battling malnutrition, disease, illiteracy, and poor sanitation on a daily basis. If nothing is done to help people in impoverished countries, terrorism and violent crime will only continue. When we fight poverty, the risk of terrorism and violence diminishes. The death penalty, already declared unconstitutional in South Africa and not permitted under the statutes for the International Criminal Court or the International Tribunal for the Former Yugoslavia, must be done away with as well.[9]

In executing people, America is already far out of step with its allies. In Europe, only countries that outlaw the death penalty are permitted to join the fifteen-member European Union and the forty-three-nation Council of Europe, the continent's leading human rights organization. The Council of Europe denounced Timothy McVeigh's execution as "sad, pathetic and wrong," and London-based Amnesty International called it a "failure of human rights leadership at the highest levels of government." In 2001, the Parliamentary Assembly of the Council of Europe even adopted a resolution calling into question the United States' observer status: "the death penalty," it said, "has no legitimate place in the penal systems of modern civilized societies, and . . . its application constitutes torture and inhuman or degrading punishment." Already, a large number of countries, including Canada, Mexico, and European countries such as France, Ireland, Italy, the Netherlands, Spain, and the United Kingdom, have refused to extradite criminal suspects to the United States if they would face the death penalty.[10]

Right now, only China, Congo, Iran, and Saudi Arabia execute more people than the United States, and, worldwide, only a handful of other countries have executed juvenile offenders in recent times. "Every one of those other countries is known for human-rights violations," notes Steven Hawkins of the National Coalition to Abolish the Death Penalty. Juvenile offenders are no longer put to death even in China, where thousands of executions take place, while nineteen sixteen- or seventeen-year-old offenders have been executed in the United States since 1985. Only two countries, Somalia and the United States, have yet to ratify the United Nations Convention on the Rights of the Child, which prohibits capital punishment for those who kill before age eighteen. Somalia lacks a functioning government to engage in a ratification process, while America—which should be a world leader in all aspects of international human rights—currently has eighty-three juvenile offenders on death row.[11]

To quench its bloodlust for the death penalty, the United States has, at times, even ignored its own treaty obligations. In 1998, the fifteen-judge International Court of Justice, the United Nations' highest judicial body, unanimously ruled that the execution of Virginia death row inmate Angel Francisco Breard should be stayed. Paraguay, Breard's homeland, claimed Virginia police violated the Vienna Convention on Consular Relations by failing to tell Breard that he had a right to consult with Paraguayan officials after his arrest for murder. "The United States should take all measures at its disposal to ensure that Angel Francisco Breard is not executed pending the final decision in these proceedings," the international court ruled. Although U.S. Secretary of State Madeleine Albright asked Virginia's governor to halt the execution, it was not stopped, and all that was forthcoming was an apology that the treaty had been ignored. In 2001, the International Court of Justice ruled that the United States violated that same treaty when, in 1999, it executed German brothers Karl and Walter LaGrand. In that case, a decade had gone by before the German consulate learned of their case.[12]

In 2000, to call attention to the death penalty issue, Italy's Colosseum in Rome—once the site of sword fights between gladiators and the persecution of Christians, who were fed to lions—was lit up for forty-eight hours every time a country abolished the death penalty or set aside a death sentence. At the end of that year, U.N. Secretary General Kofi Annan also warmly received petitions signed by 3.2 million people calling for a worldwide moratorium on the death penalty. Such vigils and petitions are emblematic of the worldwide movement to abolish the death penalty—a movement that has already started to take hold in the United States via state-imposed moratoria on executions. Although such developments might not lead to the outright abolition of capital punishment in the immediate future, they certainly could in due time, particularly if life-without-parole sentences are advocated for and if enough pressure is brought to bear both by U.S. citizens and the world community.[13]

America's death penalty will, I'm certain, be abolished one day, as it has been in Europe and elsewhere. The only question in my mind is when that will happen. To be sure, abolition will not come easily or happen overnight, particularly since executions are an age-old phenomenon. However, the death penalty's long history is marked by successive restrictions on its use and, in other countries, eventual abolition. Even if America's death penalty survives for another generation or two, it will not, I believe, last much longer than that. It will collapse under the weight of its own fatal flaws and because it makes a mockery of the law's loftiest ideals, principles such as equality and human dignity. Just consider the U.S. Supreme Court's own existing Eighth Amendment jurisprudence.

The nation's highest court ruled long ago that the proscription against "cruel and unusual punishments" requires that prisoners be given adequate medical care. The malicious use of excessive physical force against a prisoner—blows causing bruises, swelling, or loosened teeth, for example—violates the Eighth Amendment, as does "deliberate indifference" to a prisoner's safety. While prison conditions may be "harsh," the Court says, they cannot "gratuitously" allow "the beating or rape of one prisoner by another." A 1993 Supreme Court ruling even allowed a prisoner to use the "cruel and unusual punishments" clause to sue for excessive exposure to secondhand smoke where another inmate, in a shared cell, smoked five packs of cigarettes a day.[14]

Ironically, while the law protects prisoners from secondhand smoke and flogging, the Supreme Court still allows prisoners to be executed. Only if a "national consensus" has developed against a particular practice has the Court struck down the death penalty's use. Thus, in *Atkins v. Virginia*, the Court, taking notice of a slew of new state laws outlawing the execution of retarded persons, held that the execution of the mentally retarded violates the Eighth Amendment. Given the Court's emphasis in *Atkins* on "the consistency of the direction of change" at the state legislative level, if enough states abolish the death penalty entirely, the U.S. Supreme Court could conceivably be compelled one day to follow suit. If today's justices allow executions under the Constitution's Eighth Amendment because they do not feel the "evolving standards of decency" have evolved enough for the death penalty to be considered "cruel and unusual," that could change someday as society's mores evolve.[15]

Already, Justice Sandra Day O'Connor has expressed reservations about capital punishment and her own role in the process. In a speech she gave in Minneapolis in July 2001, she told the audience that "if statistics are any indication, the system may well be allowing some innocent defendants to be executed." "Minnesota doesn't have it, and you must breathe a big sigh of relief every day," she concluded. Perhaps other judges will follow suit and begin publicly objecting to the notion that they should be required to sign orders sending people to their deaths.[16]

Death penalty laws may give some a false sense of security, but only putting offenders behind bars and taking steps to prevent violence will make us safer in the end. Timothy McVeigh's execution certainly did not put a stop to acts of terrorism on American soil, just as death penalty laws do not stop homicides in Texas or Virginia or deter suicidal fanatics from hijacking commercial airliners and killing thousands of innocent people in a single day.

Although executions are kept out of sight by state legislators and the federal government, it must never be forgotten that when a democracy takes a life, it does so on behalf of its own citizens. What I find so troubling about the death penalty is that our most valued democratic institutions—the judiciary, the Congress and state legislatures, and the executive branch—all sanction (and are tainted by) the very same horrific act—senseless killing—that we so rightfully decry when terrorists or murderers commit their crimes. As the courageous mother of a murdered seven-year-old girl put it, "I don't honor my daughter's life by killing. Getting even is a pretty base response."[17]

We certainly do not hold up executioners as role models for our children, yet when executions occur, aren't all members of society responsible for what those executioners are doing? It is, after all, our own laws that allow executions to happen. Just as the NAACP successfully crusaded against lynching in the last century, those of us living in this century must work hard to do away with capital punishment. Eventually, the whole world may actually live up to the aspirations of the Universal Declaration of Human Rights, adopted in 1948 by the United Nations General Assembly after World War II. That instrument resolutely proclaims that "everyone has the right to life" and that "no one shall be subjected to torture or to cruel, inhuman, or degrading treatment or punishment."[18]

In America itself, the rising lethality and availability of firearms should be of the greatest concern to all Americans. In 2000, over 65 percent of the 15,517 murders that took place were committed with firearms, and handguns accounted for over half that total. Tragically, many of these murders were committed by a family member or acquaintance of the victim. Over 90 percent of murderers are male, and husbands or boyfriends murdered 33 percent of all female homicide victims. A murder occurs in America every 33.9 minutes, a rape takes place every 5.8 minutes, and a violent crime happens every 22.1 seconds. The South, where most executions occur, has the highest crime index—4,743.4 offenses per 100,000 inhabitants—of any region in the country. Americans are long overdue in taking the regulation of guns far more seriously.[19]

When someone is executed, it is not just a death row inmate—whether innocent or not—whose life is affected. His family—mother and father and any son or daughter or sibling—is needlessly hurt too, as are prison guards and men such as ex–Mississippi State Penitentiary warden Donald Cabana, who quit his career in corrections after conducting executions he came to see as morally reprehensible. "No more. I don't want to do this anymore," Cabana told his wife after overseeing Connie Ray Evans's execution. In the end, all of us, I believe, are diminished by using violence when it is not necessary to do so.[20]

The time for silence is past. As Edmund Burke once said, "The only thing necessary for the triumph of evil is for good men to do nothing." If more men and women stood up for basic human rights and the principles of nonviolence, I am certain that America's death penalty would be abolished more quickly than if Americans stand mute, as many have for far too long. Already, the long list of U.S. executions, dating back over several centuries, has left an indelible black mark on American history. Perhaps this generation will be the one to finally do away with death as a form of punishment, making capital punishment, for all time, a gruesome if lengthy footnote in history books yet to be written.[21]

Not long ago, I heard an impassioned talk by *Dead Man Walking* author Sister Helen Prejean, who speaks in churches and auditoriums across the country, railing against the death penalty and what it is doing to our country. The audience was with her—I could tell from their faces as I sat on the floor of the packed gymnasium next to hundreds of people sitting on metal folding chairs—because Sister Prejean does so well what so few have done in the past: tell the truth about the death penalty, America's deadly assembly line. I find her challenge compelling: it is time for all of us to do something, to act, to put an end to capital punishment.[22]

It is time to challenge the politicians who say the death penalty is needed to "fight crime." The evidence is in: it's not. By letting the killing go on, we are only making our society, my society, a more violent place. This is tragic and morally reprehensible, just as it is a sad reflection on American society that it should take the Europeans, who have nominated Sister Prejean for the Nobel Peace Prize on multiple occasions, to point out human rights abuses in our own backyard. The United States should be a leader in the field of human rights, not a violator of international law and contemptuous—as it has been—of international treaties and the global trend toward the death penalty's abolition.[23]

As for death row escapees like Martin Gurule, the notion of convicted killers on the loose—or the prospect that they might kill again—should scare all of us. That does not mean, however, that we should resort to the very tactics—murder and mayhem—employed by the killers themselves. Instead of spending enormous amounts of time and money putting people to death, maybe politicians should be spending more time making prisons more secure, keeping guns out of the hands of felons, and giving the public what it really needs—protection from criminals, not the killing of them.

Our nation's politicians—"We, the People," in fact—have the power to make change, and we should no longer allow our government to engage in state-sanctioned killing. As U.S. Supreme Court Justice Louis Brandeis once wrote, "Our government is the potent, the omnipresent teacher. For good or ill, it teaches the whole people by example." Just as surely as Clifton Belyeu's father, by raping his daughter and abusing his children, passed on a legacy of violence to Clifton Belyeu, a society that practices violence—

or fails to take constructive steps to stop it—will reap what it sows.[24]

Is it really any surprise that children who are abused by their families and then all too often ignored by society turn out to be violent and abusive themselves and end up murdering innocent people? Or that, in America's violent and gun-loving culture, where an estimated 75 million handguns are in private hands, kids make pipe bombs at home and tragic shootings like the ones at Columbine High School take place?[25]

The time has come to heed the words of Martin Luther King, Jr., who warned that an eye-for-an-eye mentality only makes everyone blind. As King wrote, "The ultimate weakness of violence is that it is a descending spiral, begetting the very thing it seeks to destroy. . . . Returning violence for violence multiplies violence, adding deeper darkness to a night already devoid of stars." For King, the solution to society's problems lay not with aggression and killing and revenge but with nonviolence. As he said in accepting the Nobel Peace Prize, just four years before his tragic assassination in Memphis, Tennessee, "Nonviolence is the answer to the crucial political and moral questions of our time; the need for man to overcome oppression and violence without resorting to oppression and violence."[26]

The time has come to end America's senseless, self-destructive cycle of violence. It is time to wipe the black ink of death penalty laws from our statute books and to end our complacency and inaction and our votes for leaders who mock the principles of human dignity. It is time to shut down the fatally flawed system that perpetuates violence and that let a Waco, Texas, jury condemn Clifton Belyeu to die. The time has come for Americans to finally rise up—cross their own razor-wire fence into the sunshine of human rights—and abolish the death penalty.[27]

NOTES

NOTES TO PREFACE

1. MICHEAL CLODFELTER, THE DAKOTA WAR: THE UNITED STATES ARMY VERSUS THE SIOUX, 1862–1865, at 58–59 (1998); WILHELM VON FESTENBERG-PAKISCH, THE HISTORY OF SS. PETER AND PAUL'S PARISH, MANKATO, MINN., 1854–1899, at vii, 43–52 (1899). The Sioux Uprising is known today as the Dakota Conflict of 1862 or the U.S.–Dakota War.

2. Christopher Smith & Avis Alexandria Jones, *The Rehnquist Court's Activism and the Risk of Injustice*, 26 CONN. L. REV. 53, 62–65 (1993); Trueblood v. Anderson, 2001 WL 883634 (N.D. Ind. 2001) (unpublished op.); Schornhorst v. Anderson, 77 F. Supp.2d 944 (S.D. Ind. 1999); Smith v. Farley, 949 F. Supp. 680 (N.D. Ind. 1996); Smith v. Farley, 59 F.3d 659 (7th Cir. 1995), *aff'g*, 873 F. Supp. 1199 (N.D. Ind. 1994).

3. JOHN D. BESSLER, DEATH IN THE DARK: MIDNIGHT EXECUTIONS IN AMERICA (1997).

4. LEWIS D. EIGEN & JONATHAN P. SIEGEL, DICTIONARY OF POLITICAL QUOTATIONS 61 (1993).

5. THE DEATH PENALTY IN AMERICA: CURRENT CONTROVERSIES 9 (Hugo Adam Bedau, ed., 1997); *Death Row U.S.A.*, NAACP Legal Defense and Educational Fund 3 (Summer 2002). Kansas reinstated the death penalty in 1994, New York did so in 1995, and Massachusetts was just one vote away from doing so in 1997. Michael Radelet & Hugo Adam Bedau, *The Execution of the Innocent*, 61 LAW & CONTEMP. PROBS. 105, 120 (1998).

6. *Death Row U.S.A.*, *supra* note 5, at 11, 27; Joseph Margulies, *Memories of an Execution*, 20 LAW & INEQ. 125, 133 (2002); Joseph Margulies, *Witness to the Execution*, HENNEPIN LAW. 5, 31 (Apr. 2001); *see also Women Executed in the U.S. 1900–2002*, http://www.deathpenaltyinfo.org/WomenExecuted.html (Nov. 1. 2002).

7. *Death Row U.S.A.*, *supra* note 5, at 3, 11–12. From 1976 to 1999, 86 percent of white homicide victims were killed by whites and 94 percent of black victims were killed by blacks. During the same time period, 51.2 percent of all homicide victims were white and 46.6 percent were black. *Homicide Type by Race, 1976–99*, http://www.ojp.usdoj.gov/bjs/homicide/race.htm (Nov. 10, 2002).

8. *Court Clarifies Death Penalty*, STAR TRIB. (Minneapolis), June 25, 2002, at A1; *Reprieve for the Retarded*, STAR TRIB. (Minneapolis), June 21, 2002, at A1; Russ Feingold & Jon Corzine, *Too Many Horror Stories*, ST. PAUL PIONEER PRESS, May 23, 2002, at 16A; *Recent Poll Findings*, http://www.deathpenaltyinfo.org/Polls.html (Oct. 30, 2002).

9. *14 Israelis Killed in Two Terror Attacks*, N.Y. TIMES, Mar. 10, 2002, at 1; James Bennet, *In Jerusalem, Suicide Bomber Kills at Least 9*, N.Y. TIMES, Mar. 3, 2002, at 1; *The Victims: A Voice on the Phone, the Life of the Party, a Father-to-Be, Bozo the Clown*, N.Y. TIMES, Mar. 3, 2002, at 15 (one of a series of obituaries of those killed in the attacks on the World Trade Center towers); *Texas Executes Inmate for a 1985 Murder*, N.Y. TIMES, May 18, 1997, at 22.

10. Jennifer Vogel, *At Death's Door: A Network of Minnesota Attorneys Is the Last Barrier Between Ruthless State Court Systems and the Executioner for Many Southern Death Row Inmates*, CITY PAGES (Minneapolis), Feb. 28, 1996, at 10; David Margolick, *Death Row in Texas Has a Shortage of Lawyers*, STAR TRIB. (Minneapolis), Jan. 3, 1994, at 4A.

11. James L. Volling, *Warren E. Burger: An Independent Pragmatist Remembered*, 22 WM. MITCHELL L. REV. 39 (1996).

NOTES TO CHAPTER ONE

1. Daniel Pedersen, *The Corpse in the Creek*, NEWSWEEK, Dec. 14, 1998, at 36; Karl Gude, *A Daring Prison Break, B-Movie Style*, NEWSWEEK, Dec. 14, 1998, at 36; Rick Lyman, *Death Row Escapee Found Dead*, N.Y. TIMES, Dec. 4, 1998, at A18; *After a Killer Flees, Texas Slams*

a Prison Door, N.Y. TIMES, Dec. 2, 1998, at A24; Rick Lyman, *Texas Death Row Inmate Pulls Off Escape,* N.Y. TIMES, Nov. 28, 1998, at A9; Susan Blaustein, *Witness to Another Execution,* HARPER's MAG. (May 1994), at 53.

2. Pedersen, *supra* note 1, at 36; Gude, *supra* note 1, at 36; Lyman, *Death Row Escapee Found Dead, supra* note 1, at A18; *After a Killer Flees, supra* note 1, at A24.

3. Pedersen, *supra* note 1, at 36; Paul Duggan, *"Dead or Alive,"* Texas *Intends to Get Its Man,* WASH. POST, Dec. 2, 1998, at A3; Michael Graczyk, *Autopsy Shows Death Row Inmate Drowned,* ABILENE REPORTER-NEWS, Dec. 5, 1998; *Death Row Inmate Recalls Escape Attempt,* AMARILLO GLOBE NEWS, Mar. 22, 1999.

4. Pedersen, *supra* note 1, at 36; Gude, *supra* note 1, at 36; Paul Duggan, *Body of Death Row Escapee Found Floating in Texas Creek,* WASH. POST, Dec. 4, 1998, at A2; Rick Lyman, *Troopers, Dogs and Helicopters Fail to Find Escapee,* N.Y. TIMES, Dec. 3, 1998, at A22; Judy Muller, *On the Lam in Texas,* ABCNews.com, http://abcnews.go.com/onair /insite/insite981201_muller.html (Oct. 30, 2002); *Steppin' Out,* ABCNews.com, http://204.202.137.115/sections/us/DailyNews/escapes 981202.html (1999); *Texas,* Associated Press, Dec. 3, 1998, http://home4. inet.tele.dk/lepan/lene/gurule.htm (Nov. 3, 2002); *Warden Demoted Over Ellis Escape,* AMARILLO GLOBE NEWS, Jan. 22, 1999, http://www. amarilloglobenews.com/stories/012299/tex_LD0649.001.shtml (Oct. 31, 2002).

5. *After a Killer Flees, supra* note 1, at A24; Graczyk, *supra* note 3; Lyman, *supra* note 4, at A22; Rick Halperin, *Death Penalty News,* http: //venus.soci.niu.edu/~archives/ABOLISH/rick-halperin/jan99/0246.html (Oct. 31, 2002); Novelda Sommers, *Autopsy: Gurule Drowned,* CORPUS CHRISTI CALLER-TIMES, Dec. 5, 1998.

6. *After a Killer Flees, supra* note 1, at A24; Graczyk, *supra* note 3; Lyman, *supra* note 4, at A22; *Inmate of the Week: Martin Gurule,* http://deathrowbook.com/weeklies/dec4.htm (1999); *Texas,* Associated Press, Dec. 1, 1998, http://home4.inet.tele.dk/lepan/lene/gurule.htm (Oct. 31, 2002).

7. Pedersen, *supra* note 1, at 36; Ren Molnar, *$5,000 Reward Offered for Capture of Escaped Death Row Inmate,* CFRA News Talk Radio, http://interactive.cfra.com/1998/12/03/78778.html (1999).

8. Jim Yardley, *A Role Model for Executions*, N.Y. TIMES, Jan. 9, 2000, at 5; David Rovella, *Court OK of Texas Law Spurs 1997 Executions*, NAT'L L.J., Dec. 29, 1997–Jan. 5, 1998; *Texas*, Associated Press, Dec. 3, 1998, http://home4.inet.tele.dk/lepan/lene/gurule.htm (Oct. 31, 2002); Michael Graczyk, *Body of Escaped Death Row Inmate Found in Trinity*, ABILENE REPORTER-NEWS, Dec. 4, 1998.

9. Graczyk, *supra* note 8; Pedersen, *supra* note 1, at 36.

10. Graczyk, *supra* note 3; Pedersen, *supra* note 1, at 36; Sommers, *supra* note 5.

11. Rick Halperin, *Death Penalty News*, http://venus.soci.niu.edu/~archives/ABOLISH/rick-halperin/jan01/0111.html (Oct. 31, 2002); *Warden Demoted Over Ellis Escape*, *supra* note 4; *Deathrow Relocation Brings Changes to Ellis, Terrell Staff*, Connections Newsletter, Vol. 7, no. 3, http://www.tdcj.state.tx.us/publications/newsletter/mayjun2000/features_v7no3.htm (Oct. 31, 2002).

12. *Warden Demoted Over Ellis Escape*, *supra* note 4; Halperin, *supra* note 11; *Deathrow Relocation Brings Changes*, *supra* note 11; Chris Fletcher, *Prison Officials Play Down Talk of Death Row Hunger Strike*, http://www.reporternews.com/2000/texas/strike/0104.html (2001); The Williams Report (Jan. 1, 2000) (newsletter published in Gardena, Calif.).

13. *Deathrow Relocation Brings Changes*, *supra* note 11; Fletcher, *supra* note 12.

14. JOE JACKSON & WILLIAM F. BURKE, JR., DEAD RUN: THE UNTOLD STORY OF DENNIS STOCKTON AND AMERICA'S ONLY MASS ESCAPE FROM DEATH ROW xv–xvi, 132, 150–51, 161 (1999); Philip Smith & Lee Hockstader, *6 Murderers Escape Virginia Death Row; 2 Are Recaptured*, WASH. POST, June 2, 1984, at A1, A11.

15. JACKSON & BURKE, *supra* note 14, at 158–59.

16. *Id.* at 161–64; Molly Moore, *2 Va. Escapees Are Captured in Vermont*, WASH. POST, June 9, 1984, at A1, A12.

17. JACKSON & BURKE, *supra* note 14, at 165–67; Tom Sherwood, *$10 Million Bonds Set for the Briley Brothers*, WASH. POST, June 21, 1984, at A20; Molly Moore & Lee Hockstader, *Va. Officials Cite Guards' Errors in Prison Break*, WASH. POST, June 9, 1984, at A1, A4.

18. Graczyk, *supra* note 8; Muller, *supra* note 4; Joel Coen and Ethan Coen, *O Brother, Where Art Thou?* (Touchstone Pictures 2000).

19. Lyman, *supra* note 4, at A22; *Death Row Inmate Recalls Escape Attempt*, AMARILLO GLOBE NEWS, Mar. 22, 1999, http://www.amarillo globenews.com/stories/032299/tex_LD0601.001.shtml (Nov. 3, 2002).

20. *Security Firms See Profit in Death-Row Inmate's Escape*, ABILENE REPORTER-NEWS, Dec. 15, 1998; *Escaped Texas Killer Still Eludes Capture*, CFRA News Talk Radio, http://interactive.cfra.com/1998/12/03/ 78561.html (1999).

21. Sam Howe Verhovek, *As Texas Executions Mount, They Grow Routine*, N.Y. TIMES, May 25, 1997, at 22; *Texas Executes Inmate for a 1985 Murder*, N.Y. TIMES, May 18, 1997, at 22.

22. Andrew Hochstetler, *Reporting of Executions in U.S. Newspapers*, 24 J. CRIME & JUST. 1, 4–9 (2001); Verhovek, *supra* note 21, at 22; WASH. POST, Feb. 26, 1991, at A4 (execution of Lawrence Buxton).

23. John D. Bessler, *Televised Executions and the Constitution: Recognizing a First Amendment Right of Access to State Executions*, 45 FED. COMM. L.J. 355, 370 (1993); Exodus 21:23–25 (this Old Testament scriptural passage is known as *lex talionis*); REV. JESSE JACKSON, LEGAL LYNCHING: RACISM, INJUSTICE & THE DEATH PENALTY 180 (1996). Many religious organizations, in fact, vocally oppose capital punishment. *Id.* at 174–77.

24. JOHN D. BESSLER, DEATH IN THE DARK: MIDNIGHT EXECUTIONS IN AMERICA 164 (1997); Mark Dennis, *Kosovo Dispatch: Crime Scene*, NEW REPUBLIC, July 12, 1999, at 18–21; Michael Mello, *Gassing the Bunny*, THE NATION, Oct. 27, 1997, at 28.

25. *Methods of Executions*, http://www.deathpenaltyinfo.org/methods. html (Nov. 3, 2002).

26. Tom Lowenstein, *The Burden of Execution*, AMERICAN PROSPECT (Dec. 3, 2001) (book review); Karl Vick, *Delaware Readies Gallows as Rare Form of Execution Draws Near*, WASH. POST, Jan. 21, 1996, at B1; *Rarity of Scheduled Execution Is Noted*, WASH. POST, Sept. 8, 1998, at C3; David Mazie, *Death Penalty Remains Alive Around World, Arousing Strong Passions*, L.A. TIMES, Jan. 16, 1994, at A2; *Capital Punishment USA—An Overview*, http://www.geocities.com/trctl11/overview.html (Oct. 31, 2002).

27. Gloria Rubac, *Why Texas Prisoners Risked Their Lives to Escape*, ASHVILLE GLOBAL REPORT, Feb. 22–28, 2001; Jason Gibbs, *Clayton Executed for 1987 Murder*, ABILENE REPORTER-NEWS, May 26, 2000; State of Texas,

Office of the Attorney General, *Media Advisory: James Edward Clayton Scheduled to Be Executed*, http://www.oag.state.tx.us/newspubs/releases/2000/20000525claytonfacts.htm (Oct. 31, 2002).

28. Christy Hoppe, *7 Fugitives Present "Unusual" Manhunt*, DALLAS MORNING NEWS, Dec. 28, 2001, at 15A.

29. *Escapee Gets Death Penalty*, ST. PAUL PIONEER PRESS, Aug. 30, 2001, at 6A; *4 of 7 Escaped Texas Convicts Caught*, STAR TRIB. (Minneapolis), Jan. 23, 2001, at A1, A6; Ross Milloy, *Corrections Report Blames Guards for Escape of 7 in Texas*, N.Y. TIMES, Jan. 21, 2001, at A12; Guillermo Garcia, *All Texas on Lookout for Escapees*, U.S.A. TODAY, Jan. 3, 2001, at 3A; Serious Incident Review, Texas Dep't of Criminal Justice (Dec. 19, 2000) (report to Gary Johnson regarding December 13, 2000, escape); Hoppe, *supra* note 28; Rubac, *supra* note 27; *Seven Inmates Slip Texas Prison, Believed Well-Armed*, http://www.prodeathpenalty.com/Escape.htm (Oct. 30, 2002).

30. Rubac, *supra* note 27; *Death Row Inmate Dragged Away After Execution Date Set*, http://archive.khou.com/news/stories/1133.html (2001); Michael Graczyk, *Guard Released, Inmates in Custody as Death Row Standoff Ends*, ABILENE REPORTER-NEWS, Feb. 23, 2000; Rick Halperin, *Death Penalty News*, June 9, 2000, http://groups.yahoo.com/group/txabolition/message/411 (Nov. 3, 2002).

31. Mark Cunningham & Thomas Reidy, *Don't Confuse Me with the Facts: Common Errors in Violence Risk Assessment at Capital Sentencing*, 26 CRIM. JUST. & BEHAV. 20, 25 (1999); *Occupations with Highest Rates of Fatal Injuries*, http://www.osha-slc.gov/oshinfo/priorities/appendixA/table6.html (Oct. 30, 2002); *Industries with Highest Rates of Workplace Fatalities*, http://www.osha-slc.gov/oshinfo/priorities/appendixA/table7.html (Oct. 30, 2002); Andrew Knestaut, *Fatalities and Injuries Among Truck and Taxicab Drivers*, CWC Online, Fall 1997, Vol. 2, no. 3, http://www.bls.gov/opub/cwc/1997/Fall/brief4.htm (Oct. 30, 2002).

32. Molly Ivins, *Texas Prison Riots Will Wait for No Presidential Candidate*, STAR TRIB. (Minneapolis), May 3, 2000, at A19; *Suspect in Stabbing Death of C.O. Nagle Identified, Investigation Pending*, Connections Newsletter, Vol. 7, No. 2, http://www.tdcj.state.tx.us/publications/newsletter/mar-apr-00/agency_v7no2.htm (Oct. 30, 2002).

33. *Soria v. Johnson*, 207 F.3d 232, 236, 250 (5th Cir. 2000); Halperin, *supra* note 30.

34. Jim Yardley, *Escape Prompts Scrutiny of Texas Prison System*, N.Y. TIMES, Jan. 11, 2001, at A14.

35. *Suspect in Stabbing Death of C.O. Nagle Identified*, *supra* note 32.

NOTES TO CHAPTER TWO

1. THE DEATH PENALTY IN AMERICA: CURRENT CONTROVERSIES 33 (Hugo Adam Bedau, ed., 1997); JOHN D. BESSLER, DEATH IN THE DARK: MIDNIGHT EXECUTIONS IN AMERICA 192 (1997); Amnesty International Web site, http://web.amnesty.org/rmp/dplibrary.nsf/ (contains links to Web pages containing current statistics and information about executions and capital punishment).

2. THE DEATH PENALTY IN AMERICA, *supra* note 1, at 11; Sara Rimer, *Life After Death Row*, N.Y. TIMES MAG., Dec. 10, 2000, at 100; Mark Pratt, *Killer of Elderly Couple Is 500th Convict Executed Since 1976*, WASH. POST, Dec. 19, 1998, at A7; Barbara Crossette, *Iraqi Executions Add Up to 1,500 in Past Year*, ST. PAUL PIONEER PRESS, Apr. 14, 1998, at 5A; *At Least 1,500 Executed in Iraq in Past Year, U.N. Report Says*, STAR TRIB. (Minneapolis), Apr. 14, 1998, at A6; David Mazie, *Death Penalty Remains Alive Around World, Arousing Strong Passions*, L.A. TIMES, Jan. 16, 1994, at A2; *Death Row U.S.A.* (Spring 2002), NAACP Legal Defense and Educational Fund, at 10; Amnesty International, *United States of America: Too Young to Vote, Old Enough to Be Executed*, http://www. web.amnesty.org/ai.nsf/recent/AMR511052001?OpenDocument (Nov. 3, 2002); Amnesty International Web site, *supra* note 1.

3. Elizabeth Olson, *Fair Penalties or Torture? U.N. at Odds with Saudis*, N.Y. TIMES, May 19, 2002, at 5; Nicholas Kristof, *Vanished Is Best Place for Omar to Be*, STAR TRIB. (Minneapolis), Dec. 31, 2001, at A13; Bruce Shapiro, *America's Dangerous Isolation Over Capital Punishment*, STAR TRIB. (Minneapolis), Dec. 27, 2001, at A17; Henry Chu, *Death Penalty Yokes China and U.S. in Awkward Solidarity*, STAR TRIB. (Minneapolis), Aug. 2, 2000, at A3; *Former Official Sentenced to Death in China*, STAR TRIB. (Minneapolis), Aug. 1, 2000, at A4; Amnesty International Web site, *supra* note 1.

4. Samuel R. Gross, *Update: American Public Opinion on the Death Penalty—It's Getting Personal*, 83 CORNELL L. REV. 1448, 1449, 1453 (1998).

5. East v. Johnson, 123 F.3d 235, 236, 238 (5th Cir. 1997); Faulder v. Johnson, 81 F.3d 515, 517 (5th Cir. 1996); East v. Scott, 55 F.3d 996, 999 (5th Cir. 1995); John D. Bessler, *The Public Interest and the Unconstitutionality of Private Prosecutors*, 47 ARK. L. REV. 511, 513 n.9 (1994); Doug Grow, *Fight to Save Man Wasn't Total Loss*, STAR TRIB. (Minneapolis), June 21, 1999, at B2; *Death Row U.S.A.* (Fall 2001), NAACP Legal Defense and Educational Fund, at 19; Beth Hallmark, *Wayne East's Request for New Trial to Be Resubmitted*, ABILENE REPORTER-NEWS, Apr. 29, 1998.

6. *McVeigh Dies in Silence*, STAR TRIB. (Minneapolis), June 12, 2001, at A1, A10; *Witnesses to an Execution*, N.Y. TIMES, Apr. 13, 2001, at A18 (editorial); Amnesty International, *Media Briefings*, http://www.amnesty. org.uk/news/briefings/mcveigh0501.shtml (Oct. 31, 2002).

7. THE DEATH PENALTY IN AMERICA, *supra* note 1, at 33–34; *South Africa's Supreme Court Abolishes Death Penalty*, N.Y. TIMES, June 7, 1995, at A3; *Death Row U.S.A.* (Spring 2002), *supra* note 2, at 10, 60; *Juveniles and the Death Penalty*, Death Penalty Information Center, http://www.deathpenaltyinfo.org/juvchar.html (Oct. 31, 2002); *The Death Penalty in 1998: Year End Report* (Death Penalty Information Center, Dec. 1998), http://www.deathpenaltyinfo.org/yrendrpt98.html (Oct. 31, 2002); *U.S.A. Executions by Year and State, 1997–2001*, http://web.cis. smu.edu/~deathpen/execyrst1.html (Oct. 31, 2002); Amnesty International Web site, *supra* note 1. "I can tell you firmly I am against the renewal of the death penalty in Russia," Vladimir Putin told European officials. "By toughening the punishment, the government does not get rid of ruthlessness," he said, "it only generates it again and again." *Putin Speaks Out Against Reviving the Death Penalty*, STAR TRIB. (Minneapolis), July 10, 2001, at A9.

8. Gross, *supra* note 4, at 1453; Ronald J. Tabak, *How Empirical Studies Can Affect Positively the Politics of the Death Penalty*, 83 CORNELL L. REV. 1431, 1433–34 (1998); Michael L. Radelet & Ronald L. Akers, *Deterrence and the Death Penalty: The View of the Experts*, 87 J. CRIM. L. & CRIMINOLOGY 1, 7–8, 12–14 (1996).

9. Belyeu v. Scott, 67 F.3d 535, 541 (5th Cir. 1995); Belyeu v. State, 791 S.W.2d 66, 69–70 (Tex. Crim. App. 1989); *Texas Executes Inmate for a 1985 Murder*, N.Y. TIMES, May 18, 1997, at 22; *Man Executed for 1985 Murder of West Woman During Robbery*, DALLAS MORNING NEWS, May 17, 1997, at 37A.

10. *Texas Executes Inmate for a 1985 Murder,* N.Y. TIMES, May 18, 1997, at 22; *Death and Texas: Clifton Eugene Belyeu, Executed: 5/16/97,* FORT WORTH STAR-TELEGRAM, http://www.star-telegram.com/specials/ 98deathrow/belyeu.htm (Oct. 31, 2002); *Killer-Robber Executed in Texas,* May 16, 1997, http://www.nando.net/newsroom/ntn/nation/051697/nation 1_12031.html (1999).

11. *Belyeu,* 67 F.3d at 536–37, 542; *Belyeu,* 791 S.W.2d at 68; *Texas Executes Inmate for a 1985 Murder,* N.Y. TIMES, May 18, 1997, at 22; *Man Executed for 1985 Murder of West Woman During Robbery, supra* note 9, at 37A; *Killer-Robber Executed in Texas, supra* note 10.

12. *Belyeu,* 67 F.3d at 537, 539, 542; *Belyeu,* 791 S.W.2d at 69, 71; *Man Executed for 1985 Murder of West Woman During Robbery, supra* note 9, at 37A.

13. *Belyeu,* 791 S.W.2d at 68–71 & n.1.

14. *Belyeu,* 67 F.3d at 537, 540; e-mail from Nancy Hees (Mar. 21, 2002), parole.div@tdcj.state.tx.us (on file with the author).

15. *Belyeu,* 67 F.3d at 537–38; *Belyeu,* 791 S.W.2d at 71, 75–76.

16. *Belyeu,* 67 F.3d at 539; *Belyeu,* 791 S.W.2d at 70–71.

17. *Belyeu,* 67 F.3d at 538–40.

18. *Belyeu,* 791 S.W.2d at 71–72; *id.* at 78–80 (Clinton, J., dissenting).

19. *Belyeu,* 67 F.3d at 541.

20. *Id.*

21. *See id.*

22. MARK COSTANZO, JUST REVENGE: COSTS AND CONSEQUENCES OF THE DEATH PENALTY 144–45 (1997); REV. JESSE JACKSON, LEGAL LYNCHING: RACISM, INJUSTICE & THE DEATH PENALTY 23 (1996); Rachel King & Katherine Norgard, *What About Our Families? Using the Impact on Death Row Defendants' Family Members as a Mitigating Factor in Death Penalty Sentencing Hearings,* 26 FLA. ST. U. L. REV. 1119, 1162 (1999).

23. *Belyeu,* 67 F.3d at 541.

24. Phyllis L. Crooker, *Childhood Abuse and Adult Murder: Implications for the Death Penalty,* 77 N.C. L. REV. 1143, 1167–68 & nn.93–98 (1999).

25. *Id.* at 1167–68, 1172, 1175 & nn.93, 99, 101, 116–17, 127; Christopher Farley & James Willwerth, *Dead Teen Walking,* TIME, Jan. 19, 1998,

at 52; *Death Row U.S.A.* (Winter 1998), NAACP Legal Defense and Educational Fund, at 13.

26. RANDALL COYNE & LYN ENTZEROTH, CAPITAL PUNISHMENT AND THE JUDICIAL PROCESS 268–73 (2d ed. 2001); Penry v. Johnson, 121 S. Ct. 1910 (2001); Raymond Bonner & Sara Rimer, *Mentally Retarded, He Faces Texas Execution,* N.Y. TIMES, Nov. 12, 2000, at 17.

27. Crooker, *supra* note 24, at 1158, 1174–75 & nn.57, 59; *compare* JONATHAN PINCUS, BASE INSTINCTS: WHAT MAKES KILLERS KILL? 28 (2001) ("Most people who have been abused are not violent. As a matter of fact, about 90 percent of people who have been so badly abused that public agencies have been called in to intervene do not require the efforts of public agencies to protect their own children and do not become violent criminals. . . . Yet a large number of formerly abused people do become violent and dangerous to society, and there is an undeniable direct link between the experience of abuse and later violence.").

28. DAN MALONE & HOWARD SWINDLE, AMERICA'S CONDEMNED: DEATH ROW INMATES IN THEIR OWN WORDS 10, 14–15, 17–18, 21–27 (1999); Crooker, *supra* note 24, at 1166–75 & nn.88–89, 116, 119–24, 130; Kacie McCoy Daugherty, *"Synthetic Sanity": The Ethics and Legality of Using Psychotropic Medications to Render Death Row Inmates Competent for Execution,* 17 J. CONTEMP. HEALTH L. & POL'Y 715, 716, 721 (2001); Jeffrey Pokorak, *Dead Man Talking: Competing Narratives and Effective Representation in Capital Cases,* 30 ST. MARY'S L.J. 420, 422, 434–41 (1999); Rhonda K. Jenkins, *Fit to Die: Drug-Induced Competency for the Purpose of Execution,* 20 S. ILL. U. L.J. 149 (1995); *Spare the Mentally Ill from the Full Wrath of Criminal Law,* STAR TRIB. (Minneapolis), Feb. 21, 2002, at A14; *see also* KATYA LEZIN, FINDING LIFE ON DEATH ROW: PROFILES OF SIX INMATES xii (1999); Michael Radelet & Hugo Adam Bedau, *The Execution of the Innocent,* 61 LAW & CONTEMP. PROBS. 105, 109 (1998).

29. Craig Albert, *Challenging Deterrence: New Insights on Capital Punishment Derived from Panel Data,* 60 U. PITTSBURGH L. REV. 321, 328 n.27 (1999) (citing Lawrence Greenfeld, U.S. Dept. of Justice, Alcohol and Crime iii [1998]); Craig Haney, *Violence and the Capital Jury: Mechanisms of Moral Disengagement and the Impulse to Condemn to Death,* 49 STANFORD L. REV. 1447, 1471 n.124 (1997) (citing studies); Cathy

Widom & Michael Maxfield, *An Update on the "Cycle of Violence,"* U.S. Dept. of Justice, Office of Justice Programs, at 1, 7 (Feb. 2001).

30. Memorandum and Order (Oct. 29, 2001), Peter J. Miniel v. Janie Cockrell, Civil Action No. H-00-4361 (U.S. Dist. Ct., S.D. Tex.), at 1–5, 108; Petition for Writ of Habeas Corpus, Peter J. Miniel v. Gary Johnson, Civil Action No. MC 00 401 (U.S. Dist. Ct., S.D. Tex.), at ¶¶ 1, 16, 17, 19–37 (Dec. 13, 2000).

31. *D.C. Sniper Suspect Yearned for Mentor,* STAR TRIB. (Minneapolis), Nov. 11, 2002, at A6; Dean E. Murphy, David Gonzalez, & Jeffrey Gettleman, *The Mentor and the Disciple: How Sniper Suspects Bonded,* N.Y. TIMES, Nov. 3, 2002, at 1, 28; *Stabbings Crack Japan's Sense of Security,* STAR TRIB. (Minneapolis), June 9, 2001, at A6.

32. *Man Executed for 1985 Murder of West Woman During Robbery, supra* note 9, at 37A. The Texas governor has the power, upon the recommendation of the state's pardon board, to grant clemency, and can also grant one thirty-day reprieve in any capital case. TEX. CONST., art. IV, § 11; TEX. CODE CRIM. PROC., art. 48.01; TEX. ADMIN. CODE, tit. 37, § 143.41(a).

NOTES TO CHAPTER THREE

1. E. D. HIRSCH, JR., JOSEPH KETT, & JAMES TREFIL, THE DICTIONARY OF CULTURAL LITERACY: WHAT EVERY AMERICAN NEEDS TO KNOW 192–93, 195–97, 199, 203, 205, 208–9, 216–19, 224–26 (1998); Samantha Power, *Bystanders to Genocide: Why the United States Let the Rwandan Tragedy Happen,* ATLANTIC MONTHLY, Sept. 2001, at 84.

2. MARK HUBAND, THE LIBERIAN CIVIL WAR (2000); CREATING PEACE IN SRI LANKA: CIVIL WAR AND RECONCILIATION (Robert Rotberg, ed., 1999); HIRSCH, KETT, & TREFIL, *supra* note 1, at 207, 210, 216, 229, 231–33, 237, 239, 243, 252, 271, 274, 276, 283, 285, 293; HENRY STEINER & PHILIP ALSTON, INTERNATIONAL HUMAN RIGHTS IN CONTEXT 7–10, 69–70 (1996); Robert White, *Justice Denied,* COMMONWEAL, Dec. 1, 2000; *One-Third of World's Nations at War, Foundation Says,* STAR TRIB. (Minneapolis), Dec. 30, 1999, at A4.

3. TOM DIAZ, MAKING A KILLING: THE BUSINESS OF GUNS IN AMERICA 8, 10, 24 (1999); Matthew Miller, Deborah Azrael, & David Hemenway,

Firearm Availability and Unintentional Firearm Deaths, Suicide, and Homicide Among 5–14 Year Olds, 52 J. TRAUMA 267, 271 (2002); Michael Bellesiles, *Firearms Regulation: A Historical Overview, in* 28 CRIME AND JUSTICE: A REVIEW OF RESEARCH 137, 178 (Michael Tonry, ed., 2001); Fox Butterfield, *Guns: The Law as Selling Tool*, N.Y. TIMES, Aug. 13, 2000, at 4.

4. E. G. Krug, K. E. Powell, & L. L. Dahlberg, *Firearm-related Deaths in the United States and 35 Other High- and Upper-Middle-Income Countries*, 27 INT'L J. EPIDEMIOLOGY 214, 214–21 (1998); Bob Herbert, *Addicted to Guns*, N.Y. TIMES, Jan. 1, 2001, at A17.

5. MICHAEL BELLESILES, ARMING AMERICA: THE ORIGINS OF A NATIONAL GUN CULTURE 1–2 (2000); Ford Fessenden, *They Threaten, Seethe and Unhinge, Then Kill in Quantity*, N.Y. TIMES, Apr. 9, 2000, at 1, 20–21.

6. Jayson Blair & Sarah Weissman, *The Biography of a Gun*, N.Y. TIMES, Apr. 9, 2000, at 18.

7. DIAZ, *supra* note 3, at 11, 24–26, 30–31, 39, 41–42, 47–49, 69–75; Butterfield, *supra* note 3, at 4.

8. JOHN D. BESSLER, DEATH IN THE DARK: MIDNIGHT EXECUTIONS IN AMERICA 186–87 (1997); AMERICAN HERITAGE DICTIONARY 1350 (2d ed., 1982).

9. John D. Bessler, *America's Death Penalty: Just Another Form of Violence*, PHI KAPPA PHI F., Vol. 82, no. 1, at 14–15 (Winter 2002); Raymond Bonner & Ford Fessenden, *States with No Death Penalty Share Lower Homicide Rates*, N.Y. TIMES, Sept. 22, 2000, at A1, A19; Ford Fessenden, *Deadly Statistics: A Survey of Crime and Punishment*, N.Y. TIMES, Sept. 22, 2000, at A19; *see also Facts About Deterrence and the Death Penalty*, http://www.deathpenaltyinfo.org/deter.html (Oct. 31, 2002); *Reported Index Crime Rate in Texas, 1980–2001*, http://www.cjpc.state.tx.us/StatTabs/CrimeInTexas/00CrimeSection_U.pdf (Nov. 1, 2002); *Louisiana Crime Rates, 1960–2000*, http://www.disastercenter.com/crime/lacrime.htm (Nov. 1, 2002); *FBI Uniform Crime Reports: Murder Rates per 100,000 Population*, http://www.deathpenaltyinfo.org/murderrates.html (Nov. 1, 2002).

10. Ruth Peterson & William Bailey, *Is Capital Punishment an Effective Deterrent for Murder? An Examination of Social Science Research,*

in AMERICA'S EXPERIMENT WITH CAPITAL PUNISHMENT: REFLECTIONS ON THE PAST, PRESENT, AND FUTURE OF THE ULTIMATE PENAL SANCTION (James R. Acker, Robert M. Bohm, & Charles S. Lanier, eds., 1998), at 160–64, 166–74, 177; Jon Sorensen, Robert Wrinkle, Victoria Brewer, & James Marquart, *Capital Punishment and Deterrence: Examining the Effect of Executions on Murder Rates in Texas*, 45 CRIME & DELINQUENCY 481, 482–85, 488–89 (Oct. 1999); Leonard Paulozzi, Linda Saltzman, Martie Thompson, & Patricia Holmgreen, *Surveillance for Homicide Among Intimate Partners—United States, 1981–1998*, http://www.cdc.gov/mmwr/preview/mmwrhtml/ss5003a1.htm (Nov. 1, 2002).

11. Peterson & Bailey, *supra* note 10, at 171–72; Sorensen, Wrinkle, Brewer, & Marquart, *supra* note 10, at 483.

12. Shirley Jackson, *The Lottery, reprinted in* THE STORY AND ITS WRITER: AN INTRODUCTION TO SHORT FICTION 634 (4th ed., 1995); e-mail from Nancy Hees (Mar. 21, 2002), parole.div@tdcj.state.tx.us (stating that Ernest Moore will be eligible for "parole review/release" on December 11, 2005).

13. Jackson, *supra* note 12, at 633–34.

14. *Id.* at 634–36.

15. *Id.* at 636.

16. *Id.* at 637–38.

17. *Id.* at 638–39.

18. *Id.* at 639–40.

19. *Id.* at 640.

20. Shirley Jackson, *The Morning of June 28, 1948, and* The Lottery, *reprinted in* THE STORY AND ITS WRITER, *supra* note 12, at 1434–37.

21. THE STORY AND ITS WRITER, *supra* note 12, at 633.

22. Michael Radelet, *More Trends Toward Moratoria on Executions*, 33 CONN. L. REV. 845, 857 (2001); James Liebman, Jeffrey Fagan, Valerie West, & Jonathan Lloyd, *Capital Attrition: Error Rates in Capital Cases 1973–1995*, 78 TEX. L. REV. 1839, 1861 (2000); Federal Bureau of Investigation, *Crime in the United States* (2000) (15,517 murders in 2000) (report summarized at http://www.fbi.gov/pressrel/pressre101/cius2000.htm [Nov. 1, 2002]); Federal Bureau of Investigation, *Crime in the United States*, Section II, p. 15 (1997) (18,209 murders and nonnegligent manslaughters in 1997, with 19,645 reported in 1996); Federal Bureau of

Investigation, *Crime in the United States*, Section II, p. 13 (1995) (21,597 murders and nonnegligent manslaughters in 1995, with 23,326 reported in 1994); U.S. Census Bureau, http://www.census.gov/ (Nov. 1, 2002); *Innocence: Freed from Death Row*, http://www.deathpenaltyinfo.org/ Innocentlist.html (Nov. 1, 2002) (listing over one hundred individuals freed from death row since 1973 on grounds of innocence); *see also* Sharon Cohen & Deborah Hastings, *Convictions Overturned, Lives Upended*, ST. PAUL PIONEER PRESS, June 4, 2002, at 1A, 12A.

23. Donald Beschle, *Why Do People Support Capital Punishment? The Death Penalty as Community Ritual*, 33 CONN. L. REV. 765, 777 (2001).

24. Richard Dowden, *Death by Stoning*, N.Y. TIMES MAG., Jan. 27, 2002, at 28, 30–31.

25. *Id.*; STEINER & ALSTON, *supra* note 2, at 211–16.

26. Todd Milbourn, *McCollum Condemns Stoning Sentence for Nigerian Woman*, STAR TRIB. (Minneapolis), Mar. 15, 2002, at A4; James Astill, *Woman Spared but Second Faces Death by Stoning*, GUARDIAN, Mar. 26, 2002.

27. Garrett v. Texas, 502 U.S. 1083 (1992); *Belyeu*, 67 F.3d at 541; Garrett v. State of Texas, 682 S.W.2d 301 (Tex. Crim. App. 1984); *Ex Parte Garrett*, 831 S.W.2d 304 (Tex. Crim. App. 1991); Charles Levendosky, *America's Death Penalty Madness Escalates*, ST. PAUL PIONEER PRESS, Apr. 29, 1998, at 9A; Charisse Jones, *Old Enough to Pay the Ultimate Penalty*, U.S.A. TODAY, Apr. 13, 1998; Morning Edition (Nat'l Public Radio, program on Apr. 22, 1998); Amnesty International, *Juveniles and the Death Penalty—Executions Worldwide Since 1990*, Report ACT 50/11/98 (Nov. 1998).

28. Miller, Azrael, & Hemenway, *supra* note 3, at 271–73.

29. *Many Homes with Children Keep Guns Unlocked, Study Says*, STAR TRIB. (Minneapolis), Mar. 31, 2000, at A6.

30. William Rempel & Richard Serrano, *Texas Guns Fall into Wrong Hands*, STAR TRIB. (Minneapolis), Oct. 3, 2000, at A9; Michael Isikoff & Pat Wingert, *High Noon on the Hustings*, NEWSWEEK, May 22, 2000, at 31; *see also* Elmer Anderson, Wendell Anderson, Arne Carlson, & Orville Freeman, *Don't Encourage More Hidden Guns*, STAR TRIB. (Minneapolis), Jan. 28, 2002, at A13. FBI statistics show that from 1992 to 1997 the violent crime rate fell 24.8 percent in states enforcing

strict concealed-carry laws, but only 11.4 percent in states with weaker laws. *Id.*

31. *Guns and Terror: How Terrorists Exploit Our Weak Gun Laws* at 3, 5–8, 13 (report published by the Brady Center to Prevent Gun Violence); *Texas Leads Nation in Number of Gun Shows, Dealers,* CNN, http://www.cnn.com/2000/US/06/28/gunland.01/ (Nov. 3, 2002); *Private Sales at Gun Shows: Your Friendly Neighborhood Unregulated Arms Bazaar,* http://www.bradycampaign.org/facts/issuebriefs/gunshows.asp (Nov. 3, 2002).

32. Bessler, *supra* note 9, at 13–14.

33. CHARLES JOHNSON & BOB ADELMAN, KING: THE PHOTOBIOGRAPHY OF MARTIN LUTHER KING, JR. 158, 222 (2000); DAVID GARROW, BEARING THE CROSS: MARTIN LUTHER KING, JR., AND THE SOUTHERN CHRISTIAN LEADERSHIP CONFERENCE 573 (1986).

NOTES TO CHAPTER FOUR

1. Michael Tonry, *Why Are U.S. Incarceration Rates So High?,* 45 CRIME & DELINQUENCY 419, 421 (Oct. 1999).

2. *See, e.g.,* Genesis 9:6; Numbers 35:33; Leviticus 24:17–20; Exodus 21:23–25; *see also* JOHN D. BESSLER, DEATH IN THE DARK: MIDNIGHT EXECUTIONS IN AMERICA 106 (1997); GEORGE HOROWITZ, THE SPIRIT OF JEWISH LAW 159–60 (1973); HYMAN GOLDIN, HEBREW CRIMINAL LAW AND PROCEDURE 21 (1952).

3. RANDALL COYNE & LYN ENTZEROTH, CAPITAL PUNISHMENT AND THE JUDICIAL PROCESS 4–5 (2d ed., 2001); A HANGMAN'S DIARY: BEING THE JOURNAL OF MASTER FRANZ SCHMIDT, PUBLIC EXECUTIONER OF NUREMBERG, 1573–1617, at 49–50, 52 (Albrecht Keller, ed., 1928); State v. Borgstrom, 72 N.W. 799, 802 (Minn. 1897); Michael Radelet, *More Trends Toward Moratoria on Executions,* 33 CONN. L. REV. 845 (2001).

4. COYNE & ENTZEROTH, *supra* note 3, at 5–6; Furman v. Georgia, 408 U.S. 238, 335 (1972) (Marshall, J., concurring); Lynn Cothern, *Juveniles and the Death Penalty,* Coordinating Council on Juvenile Justice and Delinquency Prevention, U.S. Dept. of Justice, Office of Justice Programs, at 3 (Nov. 2000).

5. DAVID McCULLOUGH, JOHN ADAMS 397 (2001); BESSLER, *supra* note

2, at 40; BLACK'S LAW DICTIONARY 1498-99 (5th ed., 1979); U.S. CONST., amend. VIII (emphasis added); Louis Filler, *Movements to Abolish the Death Penalty in the United States*, 284 ANNALS AM. ACAD. 124 (1952); *Capital Punishment Is as Old as History*, L.A. TIMES, Jan. 17, 1977, at 10; U.S. CONST., amend. V (emphasis added).

6. Furman v. Georgia, 408 U.S. 238, 243-44 & nn.4-5 (1972) (Douglas, J., concurring); *id.* at 261-62 (Brennan, J., concurring); *id.* at 321 n.19 (Marshall, J., concurring).

7. THE DEATH PENALTY IN AMERICA: CURRENT CONTROVERSIES 9 (Hugo Adam Bedau, ed., 1997); BESSLER, *supra* note 2, at 32-33, 41-46; David Brion Davis, *The Movement to Abolish Capital Punishment in America, 1787-1861*, AM. HIST. REV. 23, 32-33 (Oct. 1957); Filler, *supra* note 5, at 127-30.

8. BESSLER, *supra* note 2, at 44-46; ROBERT I. ALOTTA, CIVIL WAR JUSTICE: UNION ARMY EXECUTIONS UNDER LINCOLN 37-44 (1989); Davis, *supra* note 7, at 45-46.

9. THE DEATH PENALTY IN AMERICA, *supra* note 7, at 8-9; I STEPHEN E. AMBROSE, EISENHOWER: SOLDIER, GENERAL OF THE ARMY, PRESIDENT-ELECT, 1890-1952, at 88, 115 (1983); CARL H. CHRISLOCK, THE PROGRESSIVE ERA IN MINNESOTA 1899-1918, at 5 (1971); John Galliher, Gregory Ray, & Brent Cook, *Abolition and Reinstatement of Capital Punishment During the Progressive Era and Early 20th Century*, 83 J. CRIM. L. & CRIMINOLOGY 538, 555 & n.124 (1992); *History of the Death Penalty*, http://www.deathpenaltyinfo.org/history1.html (Nov. 1, 2002).

10. THE DEATH PENALTY IN AMERICA, *supra* note 7, at 10-11.

11. *Furman*, 408 U.S. at 239-40 (per curiam).

12. *Id.* at 251-53, 255-57 (Douglas, J., concurring).

13. *Id.* at 264-65, 269-70, 274, 305 (Brennan, J., concurring); *In re* Kemmler, 136 U.S. 436 (1890); *see also* COYNE & ENTZEROTH, *supra* note 3, at 77, 129.

14. *Furman*, 408 U.S. at 283 & n.28, 290-91, 293 (Brennan, J., concurring).

15. *Id.* at 309-10 (Stewart, J., concurring); *id.* at 313 (White, J., concurring).

16. *Id.* at 315, 321 n.19, 327-29, 359-60, 364 (Marshall, J., concurring).

17. *Id.* at 375-76, 380, 384-85 (Burger, J., dissenting).

18. BLACK'S LAW DICTIONARY 1261 (5th ed., 1979); McGautha v. California, 402 U.S. 183, 207 (1971); *Furman*, 408 U.S. at 399–400 (Burger, J., dissenting); *id.* at 465, 468 (Rehnquist, J., concurring).

19. *Furman*, 408 U.S. at 405–6, 410–11, 414 (Blackmun, J., dissenting).

20. *Furman*, 408 U.S. at 316 (Marshall, J., concurring); James Marquart & Jonathan Sorensen, *A National Study of the* Furman-*Commuted Inmates: Assessing the Threat to Society from Capital Offenders*, 23 LOY. L.A. L. REV. 5, 11 (1989).

21. Gregg v. Georgia, 428 U.S. 153, 179 (1976); Proffitt v. Florida, 428 U.S. 242 (1976); Jurek v. Texas, 428 U.S. 262 (1976); Woodson v. North Carolina, 428 U.S. 280 (1976); Roberts v. Louisiana, 428 U.S. 325 (1976); Craig Albert, *Challenging Deterrence: New Insights on Capital Punishment Derived from Panel Data*, 60 U. PITT. L. REV. 321, 346 & n.155 (1999).

22. Thompson v. Oklahoma, 487 U.S. 815 (1988); Ford v. Wainwright, 477 U.S. 399 (1986); Enmund v. Florida, 458 U.S. 782 (1982); Coker v. Georgia, 433 U.S. 584 (1977).

23. Ring v. Arizona, 122 S. Ct. 2428 (2002); Atkins v. Virginia, 122 S. Ct. 2242 (2002); Stanford v. Kentucky, 492 U.S. 361 (1989); Wilkins v. Missouri, 492 U.S. 361 (1989); Penry v. Lynaugh, 492 U.S. 302 (1989); McCleskey v. Kemp, 481 U.S. 279 (1987); *Mental Retardation and the Death Penalty*, http://www.deathpenaltyinfo.org/dpicmr.html (Nov. 1, 2002). Of the more than 3,700 inmates on death row at the time of the *Atkins* decision, approximately 200 to 300 were estimated to be retarded. Charles Lane, *Justices Restrict Death Penalty*, ST. PAUL PIONEER PRESS, June 21, 2002, at 1A, 9A. The *Atkins* ruling had a clear impact on other death sentences right after it was issued. *In Response to High Court Ruling, Retarded Man to Leave Death Row*, STAR TRIB. (Minneapolis), July 4, 2002, at A7. The Court's ruling in *Ring v. Arizona* also affects other death penalty cases. Joan Biskupic, *Jury, Not Judge, Must Rule on Death Penalty*, U.S.A. TODAY, June 24, 2002, http://www.usatoday.com/news/washdc/2002/06/24/scotus-death-sentences.htm (Nov. 1, 2002).

24. Coleman v. Thompson, 501 U.S. 722, 726, 748 (1991); *id.* at 759 (Blackmun, J., dissenting); Murray v. Giarratano, 492 U.S. 1 (1989); Teague v. Lane, 489 U.S. 288 (1989); Joseph Hoffmann, *Substance and*

Procedure in Capital Cases: Why Federal Habeas Courts Should Review the Merits of Every Death Sentence, 78 Tex. L. Rev. 1771, 1793 (2000); Brooke Masters, *A Rush on Va.'s Death Row,* Wash. Post, Apr. 28, 2000, at A22.

25. Stephen Bright, *Elected Judges and the Death Penalty in Texas: Why Full Habeas Corpus Review by Independent Federal Judges Is Indispensable to Protecting Constitutional Rights,* 78 Tex. L. Rev. 1805, 1833 (2000); Stephen Reinhardt, *The Anatomy of an Execution: Fairness v. "Process,"* 74 N.Y.U. L. Rev. 313, 318–19 (1999); Donald P. Lay, *The Writ of Habeas Corpus: A Complex Procedure for a Simple Process,* 77 Minn. L. Rev. 1015, 1018, 1047 (1993).

26. James Liebman, *An "Effective Death Penalty"? AEDPA and Error Detection in Capital Cases,* 67 Brooklyn L. Rev. 411, 417 (2001); Mark Cunningham & Mark Vigen, *Without Appointed Counsel in Capital Postconviction Proceedings: The Self-Representation Competency of Mississippi Death Row Inmates,* 26 Crim. Just. & Behav. 293, 294–95, 305–6, 311, 314 (Sept. 1999).

27. Lay, *supra* note 25, at 1047, 1063.

28. Kelly Choi, *Against All Odds,* Am. Law., Dec. 2000, at 98; *Ginsburg Backs Ending Death Penalty,* AP News, Apr. 9, 2001, http://www.truthinjustice.org/ginsburg.htm (Nov. 1, 2002).

29. Bessler, *supra* note 2, at 9–12.

30. Carroll Pickett, Within These Walls: Memoirs of a Death House Chaplain (2001).

31. Bessler, *supra* note 2, at 45.

32. *Poll: Support for Death Penalty Waning,* Star Trib. (Minneapolis), Sept. 15, 2000, at A4; Colman McCarthy, *Sister Helen Prejean Keeps the Faith,* Star Trib. (Minneapolis), June 5, 1996, at A13.

33. United States v. Quinones, Case No. S3 00 Cr. 761 (S.D.N.Y.) (JSR), slip op. (July 1, 2002), at 2, 31; Russ Feingold & Jon Corzine, *Too Many Horror Stories,* St. Paul Pioneer Press, May 23, 2002, at 16A; Congressional Record, Nov. 16, 2000, http://www.senate.gov/~feingold/speeches/senfloor/abolitionspeech.html (Nov. 1, 2002).

34. McCarthy, *supra* note 32, at A13; Emilie Ast, *Nun Decries Death Penalty as "Legalized Hatred,"* Cath. Spirit (Minneapolis/St. Paul), Mar. 19, 1998, at 3.

35. *Faces*, YALE MAG. 24 (Summer 2001); *Bush, Gore Firm in Commitment to Death Penalty*, STAR TRIB. (Minneapolis), June 16, 2000, at A6; Dirk Johnson, *No Executions in Illinois Until System Is Repaired*, N.Y. TIMES, May 21, 2000, at 14; *Illinois Governor Halts Executions*, STAR TRIB. (Minneapolis), Feb. 1, 2000, at A4.

NOTES TO CHAPTER FIVE

1. Brooke Masters, *A Rush on Va.'s Death Row*, WASH. POST, Apr. 28, 2000, at A1, A23; *Virginia's 21-Day Rule*, http://www.vadp.org/21day .htm (Nov. 1, 2002).

2. Deborah Hastings, *Capital Case Involved Tainted Chemist*, ST. PAUL PIONEER PRESS, Aug. 30, 2001, at 8A; Frank Davies, *Retrials Ordered in 68% of Death Penalties*, ST. PAUL PIONEER PRESS, June 12, 2000, at 4A; David Sharp, *Bush Backs Fairness of Death Verdicts*, ST. PAUL PIONEER PRESS, June 12, 2000, at 4A; *Bush Confident Texas' Capital-Punishment System Is Sound*, STAR TRIB. (Minneapolis), June 12, 2000, at A5; *Speech Given by Former Florida Chief Justice Gerald Kogan*, http://www.deathpenaltyinfo.org/Koganspeech.html (Nov. 1, 2002) (speech given at the Amnesty International Southern Regional Conference in Orlando, Florida, on Oct. 23, 1999).

3. Graham v. Johnson, 168 F.3d 762, 764–68, 770–71 & n.3 (5th Cir. 1999); Graham v. Johnson, 94 F.3d 958, 960–65 (5th Cir. 1996); Graham v. Collins, 950 F.2d 1009, 1014–16 & n.9 (5th Cir. 1992); Kenneth Williams, *The Antiterrorism and Effective Death Penalty Act: What's Wrong with It and How to Fix It*, 33 CONN. L. REV. 919, 925–26 (2001); *Late Appeals Fail; Graham Executed*, STAR TRIB. (Minneapolis), June 23, 2000, at A6; *Death Penalty Issue May Haunt Bush Campaign*, STAR TRIB. (Minneapolis), June 23, 2000, at A6; *Pressure Mounts for Bush, Texas to Stop Execution*, STAR TRIB. (Minneapolis), June 22, 2000, at A20.

4. Williams, *supra* note 3, at 928–32; *The Death Penalty in Texas: Due Process and Equal Protection . . . or Rush to Execution?* (Seventh Annual Report on the State of Human Rights in Texas by the Texas Civil Rights Project) (Sept. 2000), at 37.

5. Nicole Veilleux, *Staying Death Penalty Executions: An Empirical Analysis of Changing Judicial Attitudes*, 84 GEO. L.J. 2543 (1996); Aaron

Epstein, *High Court Scolds Appeals Panel for Delay in Execution*, ST. PAUL PIONEER PRESS, Apr. 30, 1998, at 2A.

6. Hugo Adam Bedau & Michael Radelet, *Miscarriages of Justice in Potentially Capital Cases*, 40 STAN. L. REV. 21, 72–73 (1987); *see also* MICHAEL L. RADELET ET AL., IN SPITE OF INNOCENCE: ERRONEOUS CONVICTIONS IN CAPITAL CASES (1992); Samuel R. Gross, *The Risks of Death: Why Erroneous Convictions Are Common in Capital Cases*, 44 BUFF. L. REV. 469 (1996); Michael L. Radelet et al., *Prisoners Released from Death Rows Since 1970 Because of Doubts About Their Guilt*, 13 T.M. COOLEY L. REV. 907, 949–50 (1996); Anthony Lewis, *Emotion, Not Reason, Behind Push for Death Penalty*, STAR TRIB. (Minneapolis), Jan. 5, 1998, at A9.

7. Samuel Gross, *Lost Lives: Miscarriages of Justice in Capital Cases*, 61 LAW & CONTEMP. PROBS. 125, 136 n.52 (Autumn 1998); Walter McMillian, *Statement of Walter McMillian to the United States Senate Judiciary Committee*, 22 AM. J. CRIM. L. 282, 283–85 (1994); Sara Rimer, *Life After Death Row*, N.Y. TIMES MAG., Dec. 10, 2000, at 100, 102, 104, 106–7; Mark Hansen, *The Murder Case That Unraveled*, ABA J., June 1993, at 30–31; Peter Applebome, *Alabama Releases Man Held on Death Row for Six Years*, N.Y. TIMES, Mar. 3, 1993, at A1; *Alabama Death-Row Inmate Is Set Free*, STAR TRIB. (Minneapolis), Mar. 3, 1993, at 7A; *Capital Defense Experts Come to Minneapolis: Minnesota Advocates Hosts Criminal Justice Conference*, HUMAN RIGHTS OBSERVER, Vol. VIII, no. 10, at 5 (Apr. 1996).

8. Eric Freedman, *Earl Washington's Ordeal*, 29 HOFSTRA L. REV. 1089, 1090–98, 1110–11 (2001); Russ Feingold & Jon Corzine, *Too Many Horror Stories*, ST. PAUL PIONEER PRESS, May 23, 2002, at 16A; Steve Mills & Ken Armstrong, *Yet Another Death Row Inmate Cleared*, CHI. TRIB., May 18, 1999, at 14; *What's New*, http://www.deathpenaltyinfo.org/whatsnew .html (Nov. 1, 2002); *see also* Gross, *supra* note 7, at 125, 127, 130 ("Since 1992, at least fifty-five defendants—mostly convicted rapists—have been exonerated by DNA identification evidence; most of them were released after spending years in prison.").

9. Joseph Hoffmann, *Violence and the Truth*, 76 IND. L.J. 939, 940 (2001); Matthew Cooper & Viveca Novak, *Bush Hits the Pause Button*, TIME, June 12, 2000, at 32; *Cook County, Illinois, Pays $36 Million to*

Four Wrongfully Imprisoned Men, NAT'L L.J., Apr. 24, 2000; Alan Berlow, *The Wrong Man*, ATLANTIC MONTHLY (Nov. 1999), at 66–68; Mills & Armstrong, *supra* note 8, at 1, 14; Chronology of the Ford Heights Four Case, compiled by Rob Warden (on file with the author).

10. Fox Butterfield, *Death Sentences Being Overturned in 2 of 3 Appeals*, N.Y. TIMES, June 12, 2000, at A21; *Fighting the Good Fight*, NAT'L L.J., Dec. 27, 1999–Jan. 3, 2000, at A10; *Death Row Executions and Exonerations*, CHI. TRIB., May 18, 1999, at 14 (chart); Mills & Armstrong, *supra* note 8, at 1, 14; Tammy Webber, *Man on Death Row Freed After Students Find New Evidence*, SEATTLE TIMES, Feb. 5, 1999; Toure Muhammad, *Innocent Man Escapes Death Row*, http://archives.seattletimes.com (Nov. 4, 2002) (containing text of article).

11. Bedau & Radelet, *supra* note 6, at 30 n.40, 64, 72, 75 n.274, 119, 167; *Innocence: Freed from Death Row*, http://www.deathpenaltyinfo.org/Innocentlist.html (Nov. 1, 2002).

12. Stephen Bright, *Elected Judges and the Death Penalty in Texas: Why Full Habeas Corpus Review by Independent Federal Judges Is Indispensable to Protecting Constitutional Rights*, 78 TEX. L. REV. 1805, 1807 (2000); Michael Radelet & Hugo Adam Bedau, *The Execution of the Innocent*, 61 LAW & CONTEMP. PROBS. 105, 116 (1998); Bedau & Radelet, *supra* note 6, at 58–64, 67–68; Gross, *supra* note 7, at 125, 134–36, 151.

13. Penny White, *Errors and Ethics: Dilemmas in Death*, 29 HOFSTRA L. REV. 1265, 1276–78 (2001); Stephen Bright, *Counsel for the Poor: The Death Sentence Not for the Worst Crime but for the Worst Lawyer*, 103 YALE L.J. 1835, 1837–38, 1843 & nn. 51–54, 1846, 1853 & n.103, 1858–59, 1867 (1994); Sara Rimer & Raymond Bonner, *Texas Lawyer's Death Row Record a Concern*, N.Y. TIMES, June 11, 2000, at 1, 22.

14. JOHN D. BESSLER, DEATH IN THE DARK: MIDNIGHT EXECUTIONS IN AMERICA 158 (1997); Bright, *supra* note 12, at 1805, 1806, 1809, 1811–12; Stephen Bright, *Is Fairness Irrelevant?: The Evisceration of Federal Habeas Corpus Review and Limits on the Ability of State Courts to Protect Fundamental Rights*, 54 WASH. & LEE L. REV. 1, 18–20 (1997); Betty Fletcher, *The Death Penalty in America: Can Justice Be Done?*, 70 N.Y.U. L. REV. 811, 824 (1995); Richard Pérez-Peña, *The Death Penalty:*

When There's No Room for Error, N.Y. TIMES, Feb. 13, 2000, at 3; Walter Harrington, *Is the Death Penalty Fair?,* WASH. POST MAG., Jan. 6, 1991, at 17.

15. *Belyeu,* 67 F.3d at 535–38, 540.

16. Jennifer Vogel, *At Death's Door: A Network of Minnesota Attorneys Is the Last Barrier Between Ruthless State Court Systems and the Executioner for Many Southern Death Row Inmates,* CITY PAGES (Minneapolis), Feb. 28, 1996, at 11.

17. T. R. Reid, *Bush's Death-Penalty Record Appalls Europe,* STAR TRIB. (Minneapolis), Dec. 24, 2000, at A8; William Saletan, *Slacker,* NEW REPUBLIC, Aug. 21, 2000, at 6; *Texas Judge Misfires,* SEATTLE TIMES, July 22, 2000, at A15 (editorial); Vogel, *supra* note 16, at 15.

18. James Coleman, Jr., *Foreword,* 61 LAW & CONTEMP. PROBS. 1 (Autumn 1998); Bright, *Counsel for the Poor, supra* note 13, at 1841; Stephen Bright, *Death in Texas,* THE CHAMPION, July 1999; *ABA Votes for Death Penalty Moratorium,* STAR TRIB. (Minneapolis), Feb. 4, 1997, at 1; Tamar Lewin, *Who Decides Who Will Die? Even Within States, It Varies,* N.Y. TIMES, Feb. 23, 1995, at A1, A13.

19. Fletcher, *supra* note 14, at 816.

20. Jonathan Sorensen & Rocky Pilgrim, *An Actuarial Risk Assessment of Violence Posed by Capital Murder Defendants,* 90 J. CRIM. L. & CRIMINOLOGY 1251–70 (2000); James Marquart & Jonathan Sorensen, *A National Study of the Furman-Commuted Inmates: Assessing the Threat to Society from Capital Offenders,* 23 LOY. L.A. L. REV. 5, 7, 14, 23–26 (1989); *see also* WILBERT RIDEAU & RON WIKBERG, LIFE SENTENCES: RAGE AND SURVIVAL BEHIND BARS 145 (1992).

21. Jeffrey Pokorak, *Probing the Capital Prosecutor's Perspective: Race of the Discretionary Actors,* 83 CORNELL L. REV. 1811, 1817–18 (1998); Nathan Koppel, *Selective Execution,* AM. LAW. (Sept. 2001), at 111, 113–14, 128; Joan Biskupic, *McVeigh Opens New Era for Death Penalty,* U.S.A. TODAY, May 9, 2001, at 8A; Sam Howe Verhovek, *With Practice, Texas Is the Execution Leader,* N.Y. TIMES, Sept. 5, 1993, at 6E; *Death Row U.S.A.* (Winter 1998), NAACP Legal Defense and Educational Fund, at 14; Ring v. Arizona, 122 S. Ct. 2428 (2002) (Breyer, J., concurring) (citing Appendix B [Table 11A] of *A Broken System, Part II: Why There Is So Much Error in Capital Cases, and What Can Be Done About It*

(Feb. 11, 2002), a study led by Columbia Law School professor James Liebman).

22. Jonathan DeMay, *A District Attorney's Decision Whether to Seek the Death Penalty: Toward an Improved Process*, 26 FORDHAM URBAN L.J. 767, 769, 777–80 (1999); Rachel L. Swarns, *In Clash on Death Penalty Case, Pataki Removes Bronx Prosecutor*, N.Y. TIMES, Mar. 22, 1996, at 1; Tina Rosenberg, *The Deadliest D.A.*, N.Y. TIMES MAG., July 16, 1995, at 21, 22–23; Lewin, *supra* note 18, at A1, A13.

23. Koppel, *supra* note 21, at 111, 113–14, 128.

24. ERIC RISE, THE MARTINSVILLE SEVEN: RACE, RAPE, AND CAPITAL PUNISHMENT 4 (1998); BESSLER, *supra* note 14, at 160; David Baldus & George Woodworth, *Race Discrimination and the Death Penalty: An Empirical and Legal Overview*, in AMERICA'S EXPERIMENT WITH CAPITAL PUNISHMENT: REFLECTIONS ON THE PAST, PRESENT, AND FUTURE OF THE ULTIMATE PENAL SANCTION 385, 397–413 (Robert Acker, Robert Bohm, & Charles Lanier, eds., 1998); Biskupic, *supra* note 21, at 8A; *Disturbing Disparities in Death Penalty Review*, ST. PAUL PIONEER PRESS, Sept. 12, 2000, at 7A; *Racial Disparities in Federal Death Penalty Prosecutions, 1988–1994*, Staff Report by the Subcommittee on Civil and Constitutional Rights, Committee on the Judiciary, 103d Congress, 2d Sess. (Mar. 1994), at 1. Although blacks now constitute approximately 13 percent of the nation's population, 41 percent of America's death row inmates are black. David Baldus, George Woodworth, David Zuckerman, Neil Alan Weiner, & Barbara Broffitt, *Racial Discrimination and the Death Penalty in the Post-*Furman *Era: An Empirical and Legal Overview, with Recent Findings from Philadelphia*, 83 CORNELL L. REV. 1638, 1651 (1998).

25. UNDER SENTENCE OF DEATH: LYNCHING IN THE SOUTH 4 (W. Fitzhugh Brundage, ed., 1997); STEWART TOLNAY & E. M. BECK, A FESTIVAL OF VIOLENCE: AN ANALYSIS OF SOUTHERN LYNCHINGS, 1882–1930, at 269–75 (1995); ROBERT ZANGRANDO, THE NAACP CRUSADE AGAINST LYNCHING, 1909–1950, at 4, 6 (1980); Stephen B. Bright, *Discrimination, Death and Denial: The Tolerance of Racial Discrimination in Infliction of the Death Penalty*, 35 SANTA CLARA L. REV. 433, 439 (1995). According to archived records at Tuskegee University in Alabama, there were 4,708 lynchings in the United States from 1882 to 1944. Emily Yellin, *Lynching Victim Is Cleared of Rape—100 Years Later*, N.Y. TIMES, Feb. 27, 2000, at 22.

26. UNDER SENTENCE OF DEATH, *supra* note 25, at 247–48; John Arthur, *Racial Attitudes and Opinions About Capital Punishment: Preliminary Findings*, 22 INT'L J. COMP. & APP. CRIM. JUST. 131, 137–40 (Spring 1998); *see also* Baldus, Woodworth, Zuckerman, Weiner, & Broffitt, *supra* note 24; William Brennan, *Foreword: Neither Victims nor Executioners*, 8 NOTRE DAME J. L., ETHICS & PUB. POL'Y 1, 2 (1994); Erwin Chemerinsky, *Eliminating Discrimination in Administering the Death Penalty: The Need for the Racial Justice Act*, 35 SANTA CLARA L. REV. 519 (1995); Fox Butterfield, *Blacks More Likely to Get Death Penalty, Study Says*, N.Y. TIMES, June 7, 1998, at 16; David Margolick, *Rarity for U.S. Executions: White Dies for Killing Black*, N.Y. TIMES, Sept. 7, 1991, at A1; RICHARD C. DIETER, DEATH PENALTY INFO. CTR., THE DEATH PENALTY IN BLACK & WHITE: WHO LIVES, WHO DIES, WHO DECIDES (1998), http://deathpenalty info.org/racerpt.html (Nov. 3, 2002); ISAAC UNAH & JOHN CHARLES BOGER, RACE AND THE DEATH PENALTY IN NORTH CAROLINA: AN EMPIRICAL ANALYSIS: 1993–1997, at 4 (2001), http://www.unc.edu/~jcboger/ NCDeathPenaltyReport2001.pdf (Oct. 30, 2002); *Death Row U.S.A.* (Winter 1998), NAACP Legal Defense and Educational Fund, at 14.

27. BESSLER, *supra* note 14, at 161; PHILLIP J. COOK & DONNA B. SLAWSON, THE COSTS OF PROCESSING MURDER CASES IN NORTH CAROLINA 98 (1993); Richard Dieter, *Millions Misspent: What Politicians Don't Say About the High Costs of the Death Penalty* (Death Penalty Information Center, Fall 1994), *reprinted in* THE DEATH PENALTY IN AMERICA: CURRENT CONTROVERSIES 410 (Hugo Adam Bedau, ed., 1997); Joseph Hoffmann, *Substance and Procedure in Capital Cases: Why Federal Habeas Courts Should Review the Merits of Every Death Sentence*, 18 TEX. L. REV. 1771, 1801 n.163 (2000) (citing Stephen Magagnini, *Closing Death Row Would Save State $90 Million a Year*, SACRAMENTO BEE, Mar. 28, 1988, at 1); Conference, *The Death Penalty in the Twenty-First Century*, 45 AM. U. L. REV. 239, 245 & n.13 (1995) (referring to studies showing that "it costs a jurisdiction approximately three times as much to have capital punishment than to use the punishment of life in prison without parole"); *Costs of the Death Penalty*, http://www.deathpenaltyinfo.org/ costs2.html (Nov. 2, 2002); *Death Penalty Facts*, http://www.in.gov/pdc/ links/dpfacts.html (Nov. 2, 2002).

28. RANDALL COYNE & LYN ENTZEROTH, CAPITAL PUNISHMENT AND

THE JUDICIAL PROCESS 404 (1994); Lockhart v. McCree, 476 U.S. 162 (1986); Wainwright v. Witt, 469 U.S. 412 (1985); Witherspoon v. Illinois, 391 U.S. 510 (1968); Marla Sandys, *Stacking the Deck for Guilt and Death: The Failure of Death Qualification to Ensure Impartiality, in* AMERICA'S EXPERIMENT WITH CAPITAL PUNISHMENT, *supra* note 24, at 305; Gross, *supra* note 7, at 125, 147 & n.103; Jeffrey Toobin, *Women in Black,* NEW YORKER, Oct. 30, 2000, at 49, 52.

29. RANDALL COYNE & LYN ENTZEROTH, CAPITAL PUNISHMENT AND THE JUDICIAL PROCESS 6 (2d ed., 2001); BESSLER, *supra* note 14, at 160; Theodore Eisenberg, Stephen Garvey, & Martin Wells, *Forecasting Life and Death: Juror Race, Religion, and Attitude Toward the Death Penalty,* 30 J. LEGAL STUDIES 277, 278–86 (2001); Samuel Gross, *Update: American Public Opinion on the Death Penalty—It's Getting Personal,* 83 CORNELL L. REV. 1448, 1451 (1998); Tina Rosenberg, *The Deadliest D.A.,* N.Y. TIMES MAG., July 16, 1995, at 42; *Summaries of Recent Poll Findings,* http://deathpenaltyinfo.org/Polls.html (Nov. 3, 2002).

30. Benjamin Steiner, *Keeping the Public in the Dark: The (Un)Availability of Public Information Concerning the Parole of Murderers,* 6 HOMICIDE STUD. 167, 168–69, 175–76 (May 2002); Laurie Berberich, *Jury Instructions Regarding Deadlock in Capital Sentencing,* 29 HOFSTRA L. REV. 1301, 1324–25 (2001).

31. Craig Haney, *Violence and the Capital Jury: Mechanisms of Moral Disengagement and the Impulse to Condemn to Death,* 49 STANFORD L. REV. 1447, 1482 (1997); Jordan M. Steiker, *The Limits of Legal Language: Decisionmaking in Capital Cases,* 94 MICH. L. REV. 2590, 2613, 2618 (1996).

32. J. Mark Lane, *"Is There Life Without Parole?": A Capital Defendant's Right to a Meaningful Alternative Sentence,* 26 LOY. L.A. L. REV. 327, 335–39 (1993); Theodore Eisenberg & Martin Wells, *Deadly Confusion: Juror Instructions in Capital Cases,* 79 CORNELL L. REV. 1, 7 (1993); Simmons v. South Carolina, 512 U.S. 154 (1994); *see also* Shafer v. South Carolina, 532 U.S. 36 (2001).

33. Peter J. Miniel v. Janie Cockrell, U.S. Dist. Ct., Civ. Action No. H-00-4361 (Petitioner's Application for Certificate of Appealability dated Jan. 15, 2002, at 7–8); Craig Albert, *Challenging Deterrence: New In-*

sights on Capital Punishment Derived from Panel Data, 60 U. PITT. L.
REV. 321, 328 n.27 (1999) (citing William Bowers, *The Capital Jury: Is It
Tilted Toward Death?*, 79 JUDICATURE 220, 222–23 (1996)).

34. William Bailey & Ruth Peterson, *Murder, Capital Punishment,
and Deterrence: A Review of Literature*, in THE DEATH PENALTY IN
AMERICA: CURRENT CONTROVERSIES 155 (Hugo Adam Bedau, ed., 1997)
("The available evidence remains 'clear and abundant' that, as practiced
in the United States, capital punishment is not more effective than
imprisonment in deterring murder."); *Firearm-Related Deaths—Louisiana and Texas, 1970–1990*, http://www.cdc.gov/epo/mmwr/preview/
mmwrhtml/00016346.htm (Nov. 2, 2002); *Minnesota Homicides 1985
to 1997*, Minnesota Planning, at 1–3, 6 (May 1999); *Reported Index
Crime Rate in Texas, 1980–2001*, http://www.cjpc.state.tx.us/StatTabs/
CrimeinTexas/00Crime1.pdf (Nov. 2, 2002); *Reported Index Crime Rate
by Offense Type per 100,000 Population, 1988–2001*, http://www.cjpc
.state.tx.us/StatTabs/CrimeinTexas/00Crime7.pdf (Nov. 2, 2002).

35. RICHARD RHODES, WHY THEY KILL: THE DISCOVERIES OF A MAVER-
ICK CRIMINOLOGIST 215 (1999); Warren Allmand, *Human Rights and Human Wrongs: Is the United States Death Penalty System Inconsistent
with International Human Rights Law?*, 67 FORDHAM L. REV. 2793, 2819
(1999); *Murders in Europe*, N.Y. TIMES, May 11, 2002, at A3; *The Roots of
Homicide*, SCI. AM., Oct. 2000, at 22; Christopher Reynolds, *Travel In-
sider*, L.A. TIMES, July 1, 2001, at L2.

36. Mathew Miller, Deborah Azrael, & David Hemenway, *Firearm
Availability and Unintentional Firearm Deaths, Suicide, and Homicide
Among 5–14 Year Olds*, 52 J. TRAUMA 267 (2002); Gary Lafree, *Explaining
the Crime Bust of the 1990s*, 91 J. CRIM. L. & CRIMINOLOGY 269, 273,
275, 290 (2001) (reviewing ALFRED BLUMSTEIN & JOEL WALLMAN, THE
CRIME DROP IN AMERICA (2000)); Augustine Kposowa, *The Effects of Oc-
cupation and Industry on the Risk of Homicide Victimization in the
United States*, 3 HOMICIDE STUD. 47, 48, 61, 63, 70–71 (Feb. 1999); *see
also Victim Characteristics*, http://www.ojp.usdoj.gov/bjs/cvict_v.htm
(Nov. 2, 2002) (Bureau of Justice Statistics posting noting that "in 1999,
63% of persons murdered were under age 35," that in 2000 "persons in
households with incomes less than $7,500 annually experienced the high-
est rate of violence of all income categories (60 per 1,000 persons)," and

that "persons in households earning greater than $75,000 annually were victims of violent crime and aggravated assault at rates about a third that of persons with lower incomes").

37. William Bowers, *The Effect of the Death Penalty Is Brutalization, Not Deterrence, in* KENNETH C. HAAS & JAMES A. INCIARDI, CHALLENGING CAPITAL PUNISHMENT: LEGAL AND SOCIAL SCIENCE APPROACHES 66–69, 71–72, 81 (1988); Ernie Thomson, *Effects of an Execution on Homicides in California,* 3 HOMICIDE STUD. 129–50 (1999); William Bailey, *Deterrence, Brutalization, and the Death Penalty: Another Examination of Oklahoma's Return to Capital Punishment,* 36 CRIMINOLOGY 711–33 (1998); Ernie Thomson, *Deterrence Versus Brutalization: The Case of Arizona,* 1 HOMICIDE STUD. 110, 117–19 (May 1997); *see also* John Cochran, Mitchell Chamlin, & Mark Seth, *Deterrence or Brutalization? An Impact Assessment of Oklahoma's Return to Capital Punishment,* 32 CRIMINOLOGY 107–34 (1994).

38. JONATHAN PINCUS, BASE INSTINCTS: WHAT MAKES KILLERS KILL? 53, 115 (2001); Vivian Lord, *Law Enforcement–Assisted Suicide,* 27 CRIM. JUST. & BEHAVIOR 401, 402, 406–15 (June 2000); Diana Fishbein, *Neuropsychological Function, Drug Abuse, and Violence: A Conceptual Framework,* 27 CRIM. JUST. & BEHAV. 139, 140, 142 (Apr. 2000); Mark Cunningham & Thomas Reidy, *Don't Confuse Me with the Facts: Common Errors in Violence Risk Assessment at Capital Sentencing,* 26 CRIM. JUST. & BEHAV. 20, 26 (1999); Thomson, *Deterrence Versus Brutalization, supra* note 37, at 111–12. Once convicted, a number of death row inmates—at least 70 since 1976—have waived their appeals and volunteered to be executed. Monica Swanson, *Consensual Executions: Death Row Inmates Who "Volunteer" to Die,* http://research.berkeley .edu/haas_scholars/pastscholars/0001/scholars/swanson.html (Nov. 2, 2002).

39. Bowers, *supra* note 37, at 69, 72–75, 77–78.

40. BESSLER, *supra* note 14, at 23–80, 84–95, 118–20.

41. Michael Radelet & Ronald Akers, *Deterrence and the Death Penalty: The Views of the Experts,* 87 J. CRIM. L. & CRIMINOLOGY 1, 13 (1996); *Summaries of Recent Poll Findings,* http://www.deathpenalty info.org/Polls.html (Nov. 2, 2002) (citing July 2001 Harris Interactive survey).

42. BESSLER, *supra* note 14, at 47–52, 59–60; Michael Madow, *Forbidden Spectacle: Executions, the Public and the Press in Nineteenth-Century New York*, 43 BUFF. L. REV. 461, 542–55 (1995).

43. State v. Pioneer Press Co., 110 N.W. 867, 868 (Minn. 1907); John D. Bessler, *The "Midnight Assassination Law" and Minnesota's Anti–Death Penalty Movement, 1849–1911*, 22 WM. MITCHELL L. REV. 577, 581 & n.12 (1996).

44. BESSLER, *supra* note 14, at 196.

45. Bell v. Cone, 122 S. Ct. 1843 (2002); Mickens v. Taylor, 122 S. Ct. 1237 (2002); Herrera v. Collins, 506 U.S. 390 (1993); McCleskey v. Zant, 499 U.S. 467 (1991) (abuse of the writ); Rose v. Lundy, 455 U.S. 509 (1982) (exhaustion of remedies); Kuhlman v. Wilson, 477 U.S. 436 (1986) (successive petition); Murray v. Carrier, 477 U.S. 478 (1986) (procedural default); Teague v. Lane, 489 U.S. 288 (1989) (retroactivity); *Statement of Walter McMillian*, *supra* note 7, at 282, 284; *What's New*, http://www.death penaltyinfo.org/whatsnew.html (Nov. 2, 2002).

46. James Liebman, Jeffrey Fagan, Valerie West, & Jonathan Lloyd, *Capital Attrition: Error Rates in Capital Cases 1973–1995*, 78 TEX. L. REV. 1839, 1844, 1846–47, 1849–52, 1857 (2000); Butterfield, *supra* note 10, at A1, A21; Frank Davies, *Retrials Ordered in 68% of Death Penalties*, ST. PAUL PIONEER PRESS, June 12, 2000, at 1A, 4A; *Death-Penalty Errors Are High, Study Finds*, STAR TRIB. (Minneapolis), June 12, 2000, at A1, A5.

47. RANDALL COYNE & LYN ENTZEROTH, CAPITAL PUNISHMENT AND THE JUDICIAL PROCESS 95 (1998 Supp.); Federal Death Penalty Act of 1994, Pub. L. No. 103-322, 108 Stat. 1959; Antiterrorism and Effective Death Penalty Act of 1996, Pub. L. No. 104-132; Coleman, *supra* note 18, at 3–4; Kimberly Woolley, *Constitutional Interpretations of the Antiterrorism Act's Habeas Corpus Provisions*, 66 GEO. WASH. L. REV. 414, 414–16, 428–29 (1998); A.B.A. Panel Discussion, *Dead Man Walking Without Due Process? A Discussion of the Anti-Terrorism and Effective Death Penalty Act of 1996*, 23 N.Y.U. REV. L. & SOC. CHANGE 163, 169–71 (1997); Stephen B. Bright, *Is Fairness Irrelevant?: The Evisceration of Federal Habeas Corpus Review and Limits on the Ability of State Courts to Protect Fundamental Rights*, 54 WASH. & LEE L. REV. 1, 4 (1997); Ann Woolner, *Capital Defenders, Critical Conditions*, AM. LAW. (Dec. 1996),

at 46–47; David Johnston & Steven A. Holmes, *Experts Doubt Effectiveness of Crime Bill*, N.Y. TIMES, Sept. 14, 1994, at A1.

48. WILLIAM MCFEELY, PROXIMITY TO DEATH (2000); Stephen Bright, *Political Attacks on the Judiciary: Can Justice Be Done amid Efforts to Intimidate and Remove Judges from Office for Unpopular Decisions?*, 72 N.Y.U. L. REV. 308 (1997); Crystal Nix Hines, *Lack of Lawyers Hinders Appeals in Capital Cases*, N.Y. TIMES, July 5, 2001, at A1, A12.

49. Wilson v. Butler, 813 F.2d 664, 667–69 (5th Cir. 1987).

50. *Id.* at 667–68.

51. *Id.* at 669; Wilson v. Butler, 825 F.2d 879, 883 (5th Cir. 1987); Malcolm Gladwell, *Damaged*, NEW YORKER, Feb. 24–Mar. 3, 1997, at 143–44.

52. Gunsby v. State, 574 So.2d 1085, 1086–87 (Fla. 1991).

53. *Id.* at 1086–87; *Gunsby*, 574 So.2d at 1091 (Kogan, J., concurring in part, dissenting in part); State of Florida v. Donald Gunsby, No. 84,977, at 2 (Jan. 11, 1996); Presentation of Hon. Bruce Peterson at the University of Minnesota Law School (Feb. 5, 2002).

54. State of Florida v. Donald Gunsby, Case No. 88-881-CF-A-X, Order Denying Motion to Vacate Judgment of Conviction, and Order Granting Motion to Vacate the Sentence of Death and Granting a New Penalty Phase Trial, at 4, 11–19 (Dec. 20, 1994); Presentation of Hon. Bruce Peterson, *supra* note 53.

55. State of Florida v. Donald Gunsby, Case No. 84,977, at 2, 9 (Jan. 11, 1996).

56. State of Florida v. Donald Gunsby, Case No. 88-881-CF-A-X, Order Denying Motion to Vacate Judgment of Conviction, and Order Granting Motion to Vacate the Sentence of Death and Granting a New Penalty Phase Trial, at 1, 6–10 (Dec. 20, 1994); State of Florida v. Donald Gunsby, Case No. 84,977, at 5, 9, 11 (Jan. 11, 1996).

57. Presentation of Hon. Bruce Peterson, *supra* note 53.

58. Steven Pincus, *"It's Good to be Free": An Essay About the Exoneration of Albert Burrell*, 28 WM. MITCHELL L. REV. 27, 28, 31, 62 & n.73 (2001); *Death-Row Rescue*, STAR TRIB. (Minneapolis), Jan. 5, 2001, at A18 (editorial); Randy Furst, *Prisoner Looks at Freedom After 13 Years on Death Row*, STAR TRIB. (Minneapolis), Jan. 1, 2001, at A1, A12.

59. Pincus, *supra* note 58, at 28–29.

60. *Id.* at 29–30.

61. *Id.* at 30.

62. *Id.* at 30–31, 33 & 42 n.35.

63. *Id.* at 40–41.

64. *Id.* at 42–44.

65. *Id.* at 44–47.

66. *Id.* at 47–48, 57–64.

67. Loyd v. Whitley, 977 F.2d 149 (5th Cir. 1992); State v. Loyd, 425 So.2d 712 (La. 1982).

68. Pincus, *supra* note 58, at 33 n.10; Williams v. Cain, 125 F.3d 269 (5th Cir. 1997).

69. Billiot v. Puckett, 135 F.3d 311, 312, 319–20 (5th Cir. 1998); Cordova v. Collins, 953 F.2d 167, 169–70, 174 (5th Cir. 1992); Joseph Margulies, *Memories of an Execution*, 20 LAW & INEQ. 125, 134–37 (2002); Joseph Margulies, *Witness to the Execution*, HENNEPIN LAW. 5, 31 (Apr. 2001).

70. Callins v. Collins, 114 S. Ct. 1127, 1129, 1134–35 (1994) (Blackmun, J., dissenting from denial of cert.); Callins v. Collins, 998 F.2d 269, 272, 277 (5th Cir. 1993).

71. *Callins*, 114 S. Ct. at 1128–30, 1138 (Blackmun, J., dissenting); Martha Dragich, *Justice Blackmun, Franz Kafka, and Capital Punishment*, 63 MO. L. REV. 853, 863 (1998).

NOTES TO CHAPTER SIX

1. Jim Willett, *89 Executions. I Was the Warden*, STAR TRIB. (Minneapolis), May 20, 2001, at A25.

2. Bob Herbert, *Inside the Death House*, N.Y. TIMES, Oct. 9, 2000, at A21.

3. Willett, *supra* note 1, at A25.

4. Gov. George Pataki, *The Death Penalty Brings Justice*, CORRECTIONS TODAY 30 (Aug. 1996); I. Reed Payne, Roger Pray, & Louis Damis, *Utah Stress Education Program Helps Staff Deal with Executions*, CORRECTIONS TODAY, at 160 (July 1990); *George W. Bush on Crime*, http://www.issues2000.org/George_W__Bush_Crime.htm (Oct. 30, 2002).

5. RANDALL COYNE & LYN ENTZEROTH, CAPITAL PUNISHMENT AND THE JUDICIAL PROCESS 500 (2d ed., 2001); James Liebman, Jeffrey Fagan, Va-

lerie West, & Jonathan Lloyd, *Capital Attrition: Error Rates in Capital Cases, 1973–1995*, 78 TEX. L. REV. 1839, 1840 n.5 (2000); Samuel R. Gross, *Update: American Public Opinion on the Death Penalty—It's Getting Personal*, 83 CORNELL L. REV. 1448, 1455–56 (1998); William Bowers, Margaret Vandiver, & Patricia Dugan, *A New Look at Public Opinion on Capital Punishment: What Citizens and Legislators Prefer*, 22 AM. J. CRIM. L. 77, 79–81, 91, 102 (1994); William Bowers, *Capital Punishment and Contemporary Values: People's Misgivings and the Court's Misperceptions*, 27 LAW & SOC'Y REV. 157, 163 (1993); RICHARD C. DIETER, DEATH PENALTY INFO. CTR., SENTENCING FOR LIFE: AMERICANS EMBRACE ALTERNATIVES TO THE DEATH PENALTY 3–5 (1993). From 1982 through 1996, in an annual poll conducted by the National Opinion Research Center, 70 to 75 percent of respondents consistently said that they "favor" the death penalty. Gross, *supra*, at 1448–49 & nn.4–5.

6. DIETER, *supra* note 5; Robert M. Bohm, *American Death Penalty Opinion, 1936–1986: A Critical Examination of the Gallup Polls, in* ROBERT M. BOHM, THE DEATH PENALTY IN AMERICA: CURRENT RESEARCH 139 (1991); Robert M. Bohm, Ronald E. Vogel, & Albert A. Maisto, *Knowledge and Death Penalty Opinion: A Panel Study*, 21 J. CRIM. JUST. 29, 34–36 (1993); Gross, *supra* note 5, at 1448; http://www.deathpenalty info.org/Polls.html (October 30, 2002). More than twenty mentally retarded death row inmates have been executed since 1977. Gross, *supra* note 5, at 1467.

7. JOHN D. BESSLER, DEATH IN THE DARK: MIDNIGHT EXECUTIONS IN AMERICA 81, 213–20 (1997); John D. Bessler, *Televised Executions and the Constitution: Recognizing a First Amendment Right of Access to State Executions*, 45 FED. COMM. L.J. 355, 368–72 (1993).

8. BESSLER, DEATH IN THE DARK, *supra* note 7, at 81; DEL. CODE ANN. tit. II, § 4209(f) (West Supp. 1994); IND. CODE ANN. § 35-38-6-1(b) (Burns 1986); LA. REV. STAT. ANN. § 569.1 (West 1992); TEX. CODE CRIM. PROC. art. 43.14 (West 1995); WYO. STAT. § 7-13-905(a) (1987); David R. Dow, *The State, the Death Penalty, and Carl Johnson*, 37 B.C. L. REV. 691, 702 (1996); Sam Howe Verhovek, *Texas Set to Execute a Female Convict; First in 135 Years*, N.Y. TIMES, Feb. 2, 1998, at A1. Arizona, Texas, and Virginia have very recently moved away from holding executions in the middle of the night, opting to execute inmates in the afternoon or eve-

ning "to reduce lost sleep for judges" and "overtime for guards." *States Abandoning Midnight Executions,* CNN Interactive, Oct. 7, 1997, http:// europe.cnn.com/US/9710/07/execution.time.ap/ (1998). Virginia moved its executions from 11:00 P.M. to 9:00 P.M., and Arizona moved its executions from midnight to between 3:00 and 4:00 P.M. *Id.* Justice Sandra Day O'Connor asked states to stop scheduling executions for midnight, stating that "dispensing justice at that hour of the morning is difficult, to say the least." *Id.* At a meeting of judges and lawyers in 1997, Justice O'Connor complained about the execution of William Woratzeck in Arizona that kept her up until 3:00 A.M. Eastern time until he was killed by lethal injection. She described the flurry of last-minute appeals as executions approached as "one of the most worrisome aspects of my job." *Justice Asks States to Stop Setting Midnight Executions,* Las Vegas Rev.-J., Aug. 20, 1997.

9. Sam Howe Verhovek, *As Texas Executions Mount, They Grow Routine,* N.Y. Times, May 25, 1997, at 22.

10. Bessler, Death in the Dark, *supra* note 7, at 9–12, 75–76; Amanda Dowlen, *An Analysis of Texas Capital Sentencing Procedure: Is Texas Denying Its Capital Defendants Due Process by Keeping Jurors Uninformed of Parole Eligibility?,* 29 Tex. Tech L. Rev. 1111 (1998); Verhovek, *supra* note 9, at 1, 22; David E. Rovella, *Court OK of Texas Law Spurs 1997 Executions,* Nat'l L.J., Dec. 29, 1997–Jan. 5, 1998.

11. Verhovek, *supra* note 8, at A14. When polls ask whether Americans favor the death penalty in specific cases in the context of particular facts, death penalty support typically drops substantially, even in notorious cases like those of O.J. Simpson or Terry Nichols. Gross, *supra* note 5, at 1471.

12. Rev. Jesse Jackson, Legal Lynching: Racism, Injustice and the Death Penalty (1996) (written with Jesse Jackson, Jr.); *Senators Vote to Condemn Bombing, Cheer White House,* Star Trib. (Minneapolis), Apr. 26, 1995, at 7A; *Changes in the Death Penalty Laws Around the U.S. 2000–2002,* http://www.deathpenaltyinfo.org/Changes.html (Nov. 3, 2002).

13. Bessler, Death in the Dark, *supra* note 7, at 137–38; Sam Howe Verhovek, *Halt the Execution! Are You Crazy?,* N.Y. Times, Apr. 26, 1998, at 4; Peter Applebome, *Arkansas Execution Raises Questions on Governor's Politics,* N.Y. Times, Jan. 25, 1992, at 8.

14. Belyeu v. Scott, 67 F.3d 535, 536 (5th Cir. 1995); Verhovek, *supra* note 13, at 4; Eric Lichtblau, *Seeking Death Penalty, U.S. May Let Virginia Try 2 First*, N.Y. TIMES, Nov. 3, 2002, at 29; Anna Quindlen, *Death-row Cases Brought Out Worst in Clinton, Bush*, STAR TRIB. (Minneapolis), June 16, 2000, at A25.

15. Gregg v. Georgia, 428 U.S. 153, 232 (1976) (Marshall, J., dissenting).

16. BESSLER, DEATH IN THE DARK, *supra* note 7, at 184; RESPONDING TO THE SCREEN: RECEPTION AND REACTION PROCESSES 229–30 (Bryant & Zillman, eds., 1991); TELEVISION AND THE AMERICAN FAMILY 3, 21–22 (Jennings Bryant, ed., 1990); Shanto Iyengar, *How Television News Affects Voters: From Setting Agendas to Defining Standards*, 6 NOTRE DAME J.L., ETHICS & PUB. POL'Y 33 (1992).

17. *Belyeu*, 67 F.3d at 536–37; *After a Killer Flees, Texas Slams a Prison Door*, N.Y. TIMES, Dec. 2, 1998, at A24.

18. BESSLER, DEATH IN THE DARK, *supra* note 7, at 157; Gross, *supra* note 5, at 1457 ("Most Americans believe that murderers who are sentenced to life imprisonment will be released in twenty, or ten, or even seven years."); *see also* Theodore Eisenberg & Martin T. Wells, *Deadly Confusion: Juror Instructions in Capital Cases*, 79 CORNELL L. REV. 1, 7 (1993) ("Jurors who believe the alternative to death is a relatively short time tend to sentence to death. Jurors who believe the alternative treatment is longer tend to sentence to life.").

19. Dowlen, *supra* note 10, at 1111, 1113, 1118–19 (1998); *Life Without Parole*, http://www.deathpenaltyinfo.org/lwop.html (Oct. 30, 2002) (listing thirty-five of thirty-eight death penalty states with life-without-parole statutes).

20. William J. Bowers & Benjamin D. Steiner, *Choosing Life or Death: Sentencing Dynamics in Capital Cases*, in AMERICA'S EXPERIMENT WITH CAPITAL PUNISHMENT: REFLECTIONS ON THE PAST, PRESENT, AND FUTURE OF THE ULTIMATE PENAL SANCTION 330–33 (Acker, Bohn, & Lanier, eds., 1998); J. Mark Lane, *"Is There Life Without Parole?": A Capital Defendant's Right to a Meaningful Alternative Sentence*, 26 LOY. L.A. L. REV. 327 (1993); *Fewer Inmates Sentenced to Life Earn Parole*, HOUSTON POST, Aug. 11, 1992 ("Last year, 205 inmates facing life imprisonment were paroled, compared with 425 in 1990.").

21. Howard French, *Secrecy of Japan's Executions Is Criticized as Unduly Cruel*, N.Y. TIMES, June 30, 2002, at 1, 6; *In Peculiar Ritual, Japan*

Executes Two Prisoners in Near-Secrecy, STAR TRIB. (Minneapolis), Dec. 26, 1999, at A8; Nicholas Kristof, *Death Penalty Popular in Japan, but Rare Recently*, N.Y. TIMES, May 29, 1995, at 2.

22. BESSLER, DEATH IN THE DARK, *supra* note 7, at 150; ILL. ANN. STAT. ch. 38, para. 119-5(e) (Smith-Hurd Supp. 1992).

23. BESSLER, DEATH IN THE DARK, *supra* note 7, at 163–82, 188–96; PATRICK BIRKINSHAW, FREEDOM OF INFORMATION: THE LAW, THE PRACTICE, AND THE IDEAL (1996); ANN TAYLOR SCHWING, OPEN MEETING LAWS (1994).

24. BESSLER, DEATH IN THE DARK, *supra* note 7, at 12–17, 164–70; Ronald Goldfarb, *The Invisible Supreme Court*, N.Y. TIMES, May 4, 1996, at 15.

25. SISTER HELEN PREJEAN, DEAD MAN WALKING: AN EYEWITNESS AC-COUNT OF THE DEATH PENALTY IN THE UNITED STATES 57 (1994); Michael Radelet & Hugo Adam Bedau, *The Execution of the Innocent*, 61 LAW & CONTEMP. PROBS. 105, 119 (1998); James Brooke, *Utah Debates Firing Squads in Clash of Past and Present*, N.Y. TIMES, Jan. 14, 1996, at 10; *Facts About Clemency*, http://www.deathpenaltyinfo.org/clemency.html (Feb. 28, 2003).

26. BESSLER, DEATH IN THE DARK, *supra* note 7, at 149–50, 152; Deborah W. Denno, *Getting to Death: Are Executions Constitutional?*, 82 IOWA L. REV. 319, 375 (1997).

27. Rice v. Wood, 77 F.3d 1138, 1139–40 (9th Cir. 1996).

28. *Id.* at 1141–45; *id.* at 1150 (Nelson, J., dissenting) (*quoting* FRANZ KAFKA, DER PROZESS 194 (1935)).

29. United States v. McVeigh, 153 F.3d 1166, 1177, 1210–11, 1213–14 (10th Cir. 1998); *In Book, McVeigh Admits Bombing, Shows No Remorse*, STAR TRIB. (Minneapolis), Mar. 29, 2001, at A14.

30. Pam Louwagie, *Execution Witness Hopes for Peace of Mind*, STAR TRIB. (Minneapolis), June 12, 2001, at A10.

31. United States v. McVeigh, 153 F.3d 1166, 1177 (10th Cir. 1998); Sara Rimer, *McVeigh's Father Recalls "Just a Kid,"* STAR TRIB. (Minneapolis), Apr. 29, 2001, at A3; *McVeigh's Dad Will Be Alone Execution Day*, http://specials.tribstar.com/mcveigh/billmcveigh.html (Nov. 2, 2002).

32. P. Solomon Banda, *McVeigh Wants Execution Date Set*, Associated

Press, Dec. 12, 2000, http://www.crimelynx.com/execset.html (Nov. 2, 2002); Eric Hafertepen, *Will "An Eye for an Eye" Leave Us Anything but Blind?*, http://www.citybeat.com/2001-08-16/bq.shtml (Nov. 2, 2002); Sara Rimer, *Victims Not of One Voice on Execution of McVeigh*, N.Y. TIMES, Apr. 25, 2001, at A1.

33. Sara Rimer, *In the Busiest Death Chamber, Duty Carries Its Own Burdens*, N.Y. TIMES, Dec. 17, 2000, at 1, 32; Bob Herbert, *Death Penalty Victims*, N.Y. TIMES, Oct. 12, 2000, at A31; Bob Herbert, *Inside the Death House*, N.Y. TIMES, Oct. 9, 2000, at A21.

34. Bessler, *Televised Executions*, supra note 7, at 358; Jef I. Richards & R. Bruce Easter, *Televising Executions: The High-Tech Alternative to Public Hangings*, 40 UCLA L. REV. 381 (1992); William Bennett Turner & Beth S. Brinkman, *Televising Executions: The First Amendment Issues*, 32 SANTA CLARA L. REV. 1135 (1992).

35. Alex Kozinski, *Tinkering with Death*, NEW YORKER, Feb. 10, 1997, at 48, 50–52.

36. *Id.* at 52–53.

37. Bob Herbert, *Death Penalty Victims*, N.Y. TIMES, Oct. 12, 2000, at A31.

38. Richard Pearson, *Tom Bradley Dies at 80*, WASH. POST, Sept. 30, 1998, at B6; *Vietnam: A Television History* (videotape produced in 1993 by Columbia Tristar Home Video).

39. Betsy Streisand, *Lawyers, Guns, Money*, U.S. NEWS & WORLD REPORT, June 14, 1999, at 56. By the sixth grade, the typical child will have seen approximately eight thousand murders on television. Susan Linn, *A Look at . . . Visual Violence*, WASH. POST, May 17, 1998, at C3.

40. *Saving Private Ryan* (Dreamworks/Paramount Pictures 1998); *Schindler's List* (Universal Pictures 1993).

41. John T. Noonan, Jr., *Horses of the Night: Harris v. Vasquez*, 45 STAN. L. REV. 1011, 1023 (1993).

42. Provenzano v. Moore, 744 So.2d 413 (Fla. 1999); Bryan v. Moore, 744 So.2d 452 (Fla. 1999) (unpublished op.), *cert. granted*, 120 S. Ct. 394 (1999), *cert. denied*, 120 S. Ct. 1003 (2000); Jones v. Butterworth, 691 So.2d 481 (Fla. 1997); *Capital Punishment to Get Its Day in Court*, STAR TRIB. (Minneapolis), Oct. 30, 1999, at A7; *Court Posts Photos of Last Inmate to Die in Florida Electric Chair*, STAR TRIB. (Minneapolis), Oct. 29,

1999, at A12; *Botched Execution Renews Electric-Chair Debate,* STAR TRIB. (Minneapolis), Mar. 26, 1997, at A4. A few months later, the Florida Legislature voted to make lethal injection the state's primary method of execution even as Jeb Bush approved legislation designed to speed up executions. *Florida Legislature Oks Execution Bill,* STAR TRIB. (Minneapolis), Jan. 8, 2000, at A5.

43. *Life Sentence for Third Man Convicted in Texas Dragging Death,* CNN, Nov. 18, 1999, http://www.cnn.com/US/9911/18/dragging.death .04/ (Nov. 3, 2002); *Condemned to Die,* ABC News, Sept. 23, 1999, http://abcnews.go.com/sections/us/DailyNews/jasper990923.html (Nov. 3, 2002); *With Two on Death Row, Prosecutors Eye Third Dragging Death Defendant,* ABILENE REPORTER-NEWS, SEPT. 25, 1999; *The Son of James Byrd Jr., the Black Man Brutally Murdered by White Supremacists, Fights to Save His Father's Killer from Execution,* http://www.webactive.com/ pacifica/demnow/dn20020709.html (Nov. 3, 2002); *Death Row U.S.A.* (Summer 2002), NAACP Legal Defense and Educational Fund, at 58–59; *King Found Guilty of Capital Murder in Texas Dragging Death Trial,* Feb. 23, 1999, wysiwyg://30/http://staging.courttv.com/trials/jasper/022399_pm _ctv.html (1999); *King Gets Death Penalty,* Feb. 26, 1999, ABC News, http://abcnews.go.com/sections/us/DailyNews/jasper990226.html (Nov. 2, 2002); *Man Sentenced to Die for Dragging Death,* Feb. 25, 1999, http: //newsnet5.com/news/stories/news-990225-133835.html (2000); Lee Hancock, *Lingering Pain,* DALLAS MORNING NEWS, June 7, 1999, at 1A.

NOTES TO EPILOGUE

1. Ellen Fels Berkman, *Mental Illness as an Aggravating Circumstance in Capital Sentencing,* 89 COLUM. L. REV. 291, 298–99 (1989); Dorothy Otnow Lewis et al., *Neuropsychiatric, Psychoeducational, and Family Characteristics of 14 Juveniles Condemned to Death in the United States,* 145 AM. J. PSYCHIATRY 584 (1988); Dorothy Otnow Lewis et al., *Psychiatric, Neurological, and Psychoeducational Characteristics of 15 Death Row Inmates in the United States,* 143 AM. J. PSYCHIATRY 838, 840 (1986); Christopher John Farley & James Willwerth, *Dead Teen Walking: The U.S. Is One of the Few Nations That Put Juveniles on Death Row,* TIME, Jan. 19, 1998, at 52; Malcolm Gladwell, *Damaged,*

NEW YORKER, Feb. 24–Mar. 3, 1997, at 132–33, 138, 140; *see also* Marilyn Feldman et al., *Filicidal Abuse in the Histories of 15 Condemned Murderers*, 14 BULL. AM. ACAD. PSYCHIATRY & L. 345 (1986).

2. RICHARD RHODES, WHY THEY KILL: THE DISCOVERIES OF A MAVERICK CRIMINOLOGIST 5–6, 11, 17, 19, 28, 34, 41, 64, 66, 103 (1999); *see also* LONNIE ATHENS, VIOLENT CRIMINAL ACTS AND ACTORS REVISITED 121–25 (1997).

3. RHODES, *supra* note 2, at 112–14, 119–21, 126–27, 130–37. A joint statement recently issued by the American Medical Association, the American Academy of Pediatrics, the American Psychological Association, and the American Academy of Child and Adolescent Psychiatry lends credence to Athens's findings. It concluded that "children who see a lot of violence are more likely to view violence as an effective way of settling conflicts." "Children exposed to violence," it said, "are more likely to assume that acts of violence are acceptable behavior." *Health Groups Join Media Violence Debate*, IDAHO SPOKESMAN-REV., July 26, 2000, at A3; *see also* Lois Weithorn, *Protecting Children from Exposure to Domestic Violence: The Use and Abuse of Child Maltreatment Statutes*, 53 HASTINGS L.J. 1, 6 (2001) ("The data clearly demonstrate that growing up in violent homes is detrimental to children, even when children are not direct victims of physical or sexual abuse.").

4. RHODES, *supra* note 2, at 313–14; Lynn Cothern, *Juveniles and the Death Penalty*, Coordinating Council on Juvenile Justice and Delinquency Prevention, U.S. Department of Justice, Office of Justice Programs (Nov. 2000), at 13; Ruben Rosario, *Head Start Now Deters Crime Later*, ST. PAUL PIONEER PRESS, May 28, 2001, at 1B, 3B.

5. JONATHAN PINCUS, BASE INSTINCTS: WHAT MAKES KILLERS KILL? 11, 17–19, 27, 67–68, 82, 84, 128–29, 158, 166–67, 208–10 (2001).

6. James Liebman, *The New Death Penalty Debate: What's DNA Got to Do with It?*, 33 COLUM. HUM. RTS. L. REV. 527, 528–36 (2002); Ronald Tabak, *Finality Without Fairness: Why We Are Moving Towards Moratoria on Executions, and the Potential Abolition of Capital Punishment*, 33 CONN. L. REV. 733, 742–44 (2001); *see also* Senator Patrick Leahy, *The Innocence Protection Act of 2001*, 29 HOFSTRA L. REV. 1113, 1113 (2001) ("There are death penalty problems across the nation, and as a nation we need to pay attention to what is happening.").

7. *Violence: An Enormous, but Preventable Global Health Problem*, Note for the Press WHA 54/6 (May 18, 2001) (http://www.who.int/inf-pr-2001/en/note2001-WHA6.html [Oct. 30, 2002]).

8. Michael Isikoff & Pat Wingert, *High Noon on the Hustings*, NEWSWEEK, May 22, 2000, at 30; Anna Quindlen, *The Widows and the Wounded*, NEWSWEEK, Nov. 1, 1999, at 98; *Guns and Terror: How Terrorists Exploit Our Weak Gun Laws*, at 29 (report of the Brady Center to Prevent Gun Violence); *About the Million Mom March*, http://www.millionmommarch.org/about/index.asp (Nov. 8, 2002).

9. Barbara Crossette, *The U.N.: Helping the Poor*, NATIONAL VOTER, Mar.–Apr. 2002, at 7–8; *United States of America: No Return to Execution—The U.S. Death Penalty as a Barrier to Extradition* 2, 13 (Nov. 2001) (Amnesty International report).

10. Peter Hodgkinson, *Europe—A Death Penalty Free Zone: Commentary and Critique of Abolitionist Strategies*, 26 OHIO N.U. L. REV. 625, 626–27 (2000); Bruce Shapiro, *America's Dangerous Isolation over Capital Punishment*, STAR TRIB. (Minneapolis), Dec. 27, 2001, at A17; *In Spain, Bush Is on Defensive*, STAR TRIB. (Minneapolis), June 13, 2001, at A1, A12; *Europeans Call Execution Sad, Brutal*, STAR TRIB. (Minneapolis), June 12, 2001, at A11; *United States of America: No Return to Execution, supra* note 9, at 1–2, 9, 11–12, 14–16.

11. Victor Streib, *Emerging Issues in Juvenile Death Penalty Law*, 26 OHIO N.U. L. REV. 725, 732, 735 (2000); *Executions Skyrocket amid China Crackdown*, STAR TRIB. (Minneapolis), July 7, 2001, at A11; Henry Chu, *Death Penalty Yokes China and U.S. in Awkward Solidarity*, STAR TRIB. (Minneapolis), Aug. 2, 2000, at A3; Jonathan Alter, *The Death Penalty on Trial*, NEWSWEEK, June 12, 2000, at 30–31; Farley & Willwerth, *supra* note 1, at 50, 52; *Juveniles and the Death Penalty*, http://www.deathpenaltyinfo.org/juvchar.html (Nov. 3, 2002); *Executions of Juvenile Offenders*, http://www.deathpenaltyinfo.org/juvexec.html (Nov. 3, 2002).

12. *Albright Requests Delay in Execution*, STAR TRIB. (Minneapolis), Apr. 14, 1998, at A4; *World Court Orders United States to Stay Execution of Paraguayan*, STAR TRIB. (Minneapolis), Apr. 10, 1998, at A7; *U.S. Cited as Violator of Consular Treaty*, STAR TRIB. (Minneapolis), July 10, 2001, at A9; Paraguay v. United States of America, Order dated Apr. 9,

1998, available at http://www.lawschool.cornell.edu/library/cijwww/
icjwww/icj002.htm (Oct. 30, 2002).

13. E. D. Hirsch, Jr., Joseph Kett, & James Trefil, The Dictionary
of Cultural Literacy: What Every American Needs to Know 163
(1988); Michael Radelet, *More Trends Toward Moratoria on Executions,*
33 Conn. L. Rev. 845, 847 (2001); Tabak, *supra* note 6, at 744, 760; Peter
Steinfeis, *Group Seeks Death Penalty Ban,* Star Trib. (Minneapolis),
Dec. 30, 2000, at B6; *Benetton Ads to Show Inmates on Death Row,* Star
Trib. (Minneapolis), Jan. 9, 2000, at A20.

14. *See* Farmer v. Brennan, 511 U.S. 825, 834 (1994); Helling v. McKin-
ney, 509 U.S. 25, 35 (1993); Hudson v. McMillian, 503 U.S. 1, 9–10 (1992);
Estelle v. Gamble, 429 U.S. 97, 103 (1976).

15. Atkins v. Virginia, 122 S. Ct. 2242 (2002); Jackson v. Bishop, 404
F.2d 571 (8th Cir. 1968).

16. Barbara Jones, *Justice Sandra Day O'Connor Puts MWL in National Spotlight,* Minnesota Law., July 9, 2001, at 1, 12; Maria Elena
Baca, *O'Connor Critical of Death Penalty,* Star Trib. (Minneapolis), July 3,
2001, at A1, A10.

17. Wayne Logan, *Declaring Life at the Crossroads of Death: Victims'
Anti-Death Penalty Views and Prosecutors' Charging Decisions,* 18
Crim. Just. Ethics 41, 42 (Summer/Fall 1999).

18. Universal Declaration of Human Rights, art. 3 & art. 5 (1948); Toni
Fine, *Moratorium 2000: An International Dialogue Toward a Ban on
Capital Punishment,* 30 Colum. Hum. Rts. L. Rev. 421, 423 (1999).

19. *Crime in the United States,* http://www.fbi.gov/pressrel/
pressrel01/cius2000.htm (Oct. 30, 2002) (FBI press release); Federal Bureau
of Investigation, *Crime in the United States* (2000), Section I, pp. 4, 6.

20. Donald Cabana, Death at Midnight: The Confession of an
Executioner 186–93 (1996); I. Reed Payne, Roger T. Pray, & Louis F.
Damis, *Utah Stress Education Program Helps Staff Deal with Executions,* Corrections Today, July 1990, at 160–68; Steven Hawkins, *Death
at Midnight . . . Hope at Sunrise,* Corrections Today, Aug. 1996, at 31.

21. John Bartlett, Familiar Quotations 332 (16th ed., 1992).

22. Sister Helen Prejean, Dead Man Walking: An Eyewitness Account of the Death Penalty in the United States (1994); Nolan Zavoral, *Easter Comes Early,* Star Trib. (Minneapolis), Mar. 28, 1998, at B1.

23. Fine, *supra* note 18, at 434–35; Charles Levendosky, *America's Death Penalty Madness Escalates,* ST. PAUL PIONEER PRESS, Apr. 29, 1998, at 9A; Zavoral, *supra* note 22, at B1; David Stout, *U.S. Executions Draw Scorn from Abroad,* N.Y. TIMES, Mar. 26, 1998, at 4; Emilie Ast, *Nun Decries Death Penalty as "Legalized Hatred,"* CATH. SPIRIT (Minneapolis/St. Paul), Mar. 19, 1998, at 3.

24. *Belyeu,* 67 F.3d at 535.

25. Mary Jordan, *Japan Clamors for Stricter Gun Laws,* WASH. POST, Mar. 16, 1997, at A23. Roughly 2,000 children die each year from abuse or neglect by parents or caretakers and 18,000 are permanently disabled. *See* U.S. ADVISORY BOARD ON CHILD ABUSE & NEGLECT, U.S. DEP'T OF HEALTH & HUMAN SERVICES, A NATION'S SHAME: FATAL CHILD ABUSE AND NEGLECT IN THE UNITED STATES, at xxiii, xxv (1995).

26. MARTIN LUTHER KING, JR., WHERE DO WE GO FROM HERE: CHAOS OR COMMUNITY? 62–63 (1967); Martin Luther King, Jr., speech accepting the Nobel Peace Prize, Dec. 11, 1964; *Famous Quotes,* http://web.starlinx.com/nawa3em/Quotes.html (Oct. 30, 2002).

27. *Belyeu,* 67 F.3d at 536.

INDEX